ST PETER PORT

People and Places

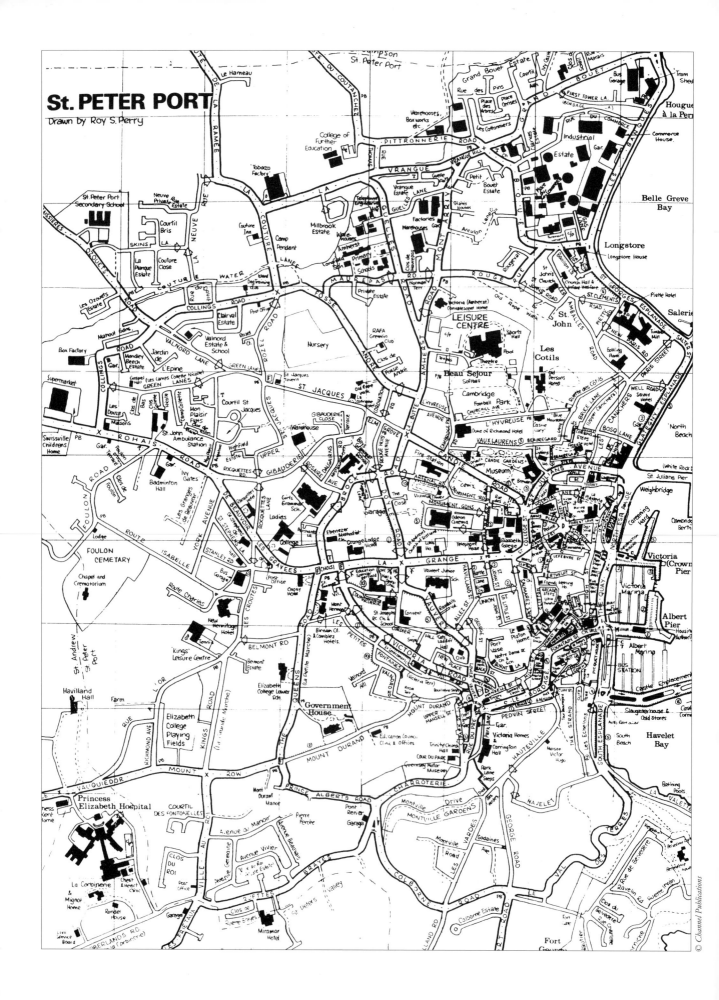

St. PETER PORT

Drawn by Roy S. Perry

ST PETER PORT

People and Places

CAREL TOMS

PHILLIMORE

2003

Published by
PHILLIMORE & CO. LTD
Shopwyke Manor Barn, Chichester, West Sussex, England

ISBN 1 86077 258 7

Printed and bound in Great Britain by
BIDDLES LTD
King's Lynn, Norfolk

CONTENTS

FOREWORD

To anyone unfamiliar with St Peter Port, this book illustrates just what changes have taken place in a relatively short time. Fortunately there are physical limitations to what can be accomplished. There are the steep valleys which run from west to east in which water mills were once rumbling and wash places where chattering women were at work.

These valleys and escarpments have buildings perched on them at different angles which make St Peter Port what it is today: a town with surprising and unexpected glimpses of the sea. A town with a cathedral-like church, with its feet in the sea, at the centre of it all. A remarkable market and square with a library. A narrow, winding High Street leading to the Constables' Office, the administrative offices of the town. And the dual-purpose Royal Court, which is the centre of the States government.

Old-fashioned industries have disappeared or moved out of town to be replaced by financial institutions and banks. But despite all this the views of St Peter Port do not change. They remain to be discovered. There are sudden flights of steps which lead ever upward or downward. There are the narrowest of alleyways leading apparently nowhere. It is only when you reach the top or bottom of them that you realise how St Peter Port was built: by people who had no option but to follow the contours of the cliffs.

Walk back from Castle Cornet to the town and you will see the whole panorama before you: church spires against the skyline; buildings at different angles and different heights. All this beauty is embraced in the arms of St Peter Port harbour with the fishing boats, the yachts and commercial craft amid the glitter of the clear blue sea.

CAREL TOMS

Acknowledgments

Grateful thanks are due to Channel Publications (Barry Wells, Managing Director) for generously allowing the use of their map of St Peter Port (Roy S. Perry) in this book. All illustrations are from the Carel Toms Collection. The following photographers are acknowledged: Garnier Arsène; T. Bramley; Peter Brehaut; John Brenton; Banks Brownsey; L.R. Cohen; B. Collenette; Geoff Dovey; Brian Green; Norman Grut; F.W. Guerin; B.E.M. Hassall; T.B. Hutton; Ave Jelley; T.M. Mansell; A.H. Marquand; Rose de la Rue; George Symons.

INTRODUCTION

by John McCormack, FSA

Gloriously situated within sight of all the other Channel Islands, Guernsey arguably owes its historic and prehistoric importance to the fact that it is hardly visible from the coast of France. For, set far out at sea, it was ideally suited to assist coastal shipping moving up and down the Channel without losing sight of land, enabling it to avoid the huge tides of the shallow waters, reefs and rocks towards Mont St Michel and St Malo, and, to some extent, the dreadful currents further north around Alderney. Yet the west coast of Guernsey is also a navigational nightmare, and must always have been so, regardless of the extent of erosion in past ages: tempting bays for beaching boats there might be, but in fact these bays have some of the most dangerous approaches imaginable, safe only for local fishermen who have been brought up to know every underwater pinnacle at every state of the tide. But the south and east of the island are different. South-coast cliffs drop straight into deep water, largely unencumbered by hazards, and then, as they turn towards the east, the same applies. And it is here that to the geographical attraction of the island as a whole is added a particular topographical felicity, because, sheltered from the worst of prevailing westerly winds, the cliffs fall back for a while to more gentle hills, forming an ideal anchorage and a sloping shore for hauling up boats away from stormy seas.

In this perfect spot grew up St Peter Port. To its lure as a harbour was added the fresh water of two streams, one short, one long. The short stream began as a spring in the Vauxlaurens – the valleys of St Laurence – and ran down Le Truchot at the northern end of the settlement. To the south, the longer stream collected water from several sources but basically originated underneath St Martin's church, and, flowing down La Charroterie, Mill Street and Fountain Street, came, in the course of centuries, to turn various mills before reaching the sea by the Town Church. Along the shore between these two streams was a low hill, partly formed from a consolidated sand dune, up which, in the fullness of time, rose High Street from the south and Le Pollet from the north. On the low summit where they met was Le Grand Carrefour (the big crossroads), and at this point Smith Street led off inland at right-angles.

Within this small compass lay, as far as we can tell, an important prehistoric settlement and the whole of a Roman port. Of prehistoric remains, a large variety of artefacts, both onshore and offshore and an occasional monument of a more substantial nature give us only clues about inhabitants and traders, but for the Roman period the last thirty years have not only identified at least three wrecks near the present harbour mouth, of which one has been raised and will in due course be displayed in a new museum, but on land, several warehouses, rich in finds, discovered by archaeologists between Le Pollet and Le Truchot. The imminent redevelopment of The Markets has given opportunity for investigations there to reveal more Roman buildings near the Town Church. Throughout the town, centuries of unrecorded discoveries and commercial rebuildings have doubtless obliterated virtually everything else that once existed from such remote ages, but what comparatively tiny portions of the settlement have so far been found provide enough evidence to demonstrate that St Peter Port is aptly named: the town does indeed owe its very existence, and an importance out of all proportion to its size, to its mariners and to its commerce.

The Romans gave St Peter Port more than a town and an anchorage of repute: they gave it a parish. We are unlikely ever to have much idea how the island as a whole was organised and ruled in pre-Roman times, but we can be fairly certain that the outlines of Guernsey's parish system reflect, no doubt in some much-mutilated way, the Roman love of order when it came to collecting taxes. For just as medieval bishoprics in France faithfully reflect the sub-divisions of provinces along those lines, so Christianity, when it became the official religion in the fourth century, utilised pre-existing patterns in the countryside. Into these were later intruded in the Channel Islands other boundaries, centred on shrines set up by Celtic saints of the sixth century, reinforcing the pre-existing Christian presence with their own evangelisation and dedications. St Sampson's, to the north, thus commemorates Guernsey's 'patron saint', of Welsh origins: but the Town Church, at the centre of St Peter Port, has a dedication typically Roman, indeed remembering the first Pope of Rome.

But though the parish of St Peter Port had its own luxuriant hinterland of pastures and arable, even by medieval times it did not officially have the island's market. This was held roughly in the centre of Guernsey, at Les Landes du Marché, on a line that is another very ancient boundary, not only, eventually, between parishes, but between feudal fiefs. However, an increased importance of the town in island affairs during the 12th and 13th centuries, partly reflecting a population growth affecting most of Europe, led to its transference with royal agreement to the top of Smith Street in 1309 and to its migration to the churchyard of the Town Church shortly afterwards. Stalls set up to attract the faithful, especially on church feast-days, were a common feature around any medieval church, especially those in urban areas. And the fees which it was possible to charge, when stallholders found it worthwhile to build permanent shops on church land, were no doubt welcome supplements to religious endowments. Already in 1309 the mixture of sacred and secular was producing so much noise that the courts had to insist upon regulation of the markets during actual services. But eventually the clutter of shops pressed so hard on the Town Church that it was virtually surrounded by buildings and, even with most of them removed over the last two hundred years, we are still left with a public house closer to the church than any in England, so it is said.

The haphazard establishment of shops on the former churchyard interrupted the clear lines of older roads. By medieval times, to the settlement of High Street and Le Pollet to the north had been added Cornet Street to the south, climbing from the Town Church up the spine of land between the sea and the Fountain Street – Bordage valley. Along these three roads, and also up Smith Street and Berthelot Street for a short distance, buildings were laid out in 'burgage strips' as they have been called in England, whether organised in one or more campaigns or whether arrived at by convention over centuries we do not know. Their narrow street frontages crammed in as many commercial premises as possible, whilst living quarters or ancillary stores stretched far back from the road. This led to St Peter Port's very characteristic appearance, its houses all gable-end on to streets, utterly different from most island farmhouses. And, as the town grew into a distinct community, it organised different inheritance laws from the rest of the island, allowing for the equal division of property between heirs, Town for this purpose technically comprising the area within walls that Edward III had twice ordered to be built, but more probably –

since no sign of any town wall has ever been found – just within strictly controlled legal limits. These were visually defined in 1700 by the erection of the 'Barrières de la Ville' stones and it is clear that, even by then, development outside these limits was minimal.

The earliest suburb was along the coast northwards from the bottom of Le Pollet towards Glategny and La Salerie. Here it was that fish was salted, especially conger eels, and exported to the vineyards of Gascony to supplement the diets of farmers who had given up cereal farming for wine-producing. For during the 12th century the islands were also part of the extensive French empire of the Angevin kings of England, and all wine brought from Bordeaux and neighbouring parts by ship to British ports came through Guernsey. Then in 1204 came the loss by King John to Philippe Auguste of France of mainland Normandy. This is a date even more vital to Channel Island history than 1066. For suddenly they became not only of commercial but of strategic importance, a crucial link with English possessions overseas and, in due course, a base from which to harry French shipping in time of war. It was then that Castle Cornet was fortified for the first time, guarding the harbour and the entire island.

Channel Islanders made the most of their new situation as frontier territories. Unexpectedly, a whole century of peace and prosperity followed 1204, and Guernseymen played their cards cannily, establishing a large measure of independence under pretext of ancient Norman rights and privileges, leading, eventually, to the emergence of the Royal Court with its distinctive sets of laws, interpreted by local jurats, to the dignity of the office of Bailiff as head of the island's legislature and judicature, and also to a system whereby the Crown exercised control through Wardens of the Isles, later Governors, or more usually through the captains or lieutenants to whom they delegated their responsibilities. Since the 19th century Guernsey and Jersey have each had separate Lieutenant-Governors and the office of Governor has been abolished, whilst the British Government deals with external affairs and contentious issues first through the Privy Council and now through a Cabinet minister, but without direct representation in Parliament.

By the 14th century, St Peter Port had become a thriving town, complete with two of its own fortifications, La Tour Gand near La Plaiderie at the bottom of Le Pollet, a tower whose unlikely name is probably derived from Ghent by connection with John of Gaunt, son of Edward III, and whose exact location has long been forgotten; and La Tour Beauregard, situated at the top of Cornet Street, demolished for the construction of St Barnabas' Church, but whose gate, the only 'town gate' of which we have certain proof, was functioning at the end of the 16th century partly as a small prison. A 14th-century town ditch ran from it down the line of Cliff Street to the cliff edge, where steps now go down from The Strand to the South Esplanade.

But this ditch had fallen out of use by 1600, and in the next few years the houses on the south side of Cliff Street grew up, the first of another small suburb around Lower Hauteville, matched in the valley below by a larger group of houses beyond Le Bordage, forming Mill Street and Contrée Mansell up as far as the later Trinity Square.

Though the stone side walls of Town burgage plots often survive from the 13th century onwards, the gabled frontages onto the streets, timber-framed and 'jettied', i.e. with overhanging upper storeys, have all disappeared. Some in Berthelot Street have been rebuilt as replicas, and the former Trustee Savings Bank on the corner of that street and High Street has side walls of around 1500. But in its present form it bears little resemblance to its medieval beginnings, for its top storeys, projecting on two sides, have been removed, its vaulted cellars broken into and its interior completely gutted. Alterations and rebuildings everywhere have been carried out from the earliest times, but it was not until the late 17th century that the actual form of houses began to change. Drawings of that time still show a mainly medieval town, and even in *c.*1720 most houses were still jettied. But by the end of that century, St Peter Port was already a vastly different town.

There had always been a manor in the midst of Town. The Le Marchant family gave their name to the short street that begins under the arch opposite Boots chemists in High Street and goes up to Court Row, where Manor Place also remembers the estate. Their actual house was rebuilt in 1787 and is now the Town Constables' Office, facing a courtyard as its medieval predecessor must have done: the chapel attached to the manor house has disappeared and the arched entrance to the street has also been rebuilt, but it is significant that the family still wished to retain a Town house even at the end of the 18th century. Many other prosperous local families also built or rebuilt houses along the High Street and in Le Pollet. The Brock house, now Boots, and the de Saumarez house now *Moore's Hotel* are but two examples of the stylish residences that adorned the town by 1800. And in Le Bordage, Le Brasserie, illustrated in this book, was a particularly splendid house built by the Carey family, unfortunately demolished in 1968.

These families had made their fortunes in various ways, but one of the most lucrative, from the end of the 17th century onwards, was to own a privateer and prey on enemy shipping. These 'licensed pirates' often captured fabulous prizes on the high seas. The importance of St Peter Port as an entrepôt also began at this time and goods held in bond for transhipment elsewhere became very profitable and led to the building of large warehouses. Merchants also had their representatives, often relatives, in English towns – London, Poole, Southampton, Bristol – and on the Continent in almost every country at various times. Contact with the New World was also continuous, and Guernseymen found themselves on voyages of exploration around the globe and involved in every colony and every colonial war. It was a Guernseyman who designed the first uniform for the Royal Navy and another who founded Sandhurst.

The construction of the harbour, where boats could tie up at quays, as distinct from being dragged up the beach or anchored off shore, was first put in hand during the great expansion of St Peter Port in the 13th century, and was certainly in existence by 1294, when it was damaged in the French raid of that year, which also destroyed part of the Town Church. This was the origin of the South Quay, which was completely rebuilt in 1590. A low northern arm existed by the 17th century, but is shown in 1680 as submerged during high tides, and it was not reconstructed as a proper pier until 1750. There was still no wharf on the landward side and to pass between the two arms of the Old Harbour one walked along the beach. The Coal Quay, as it was first called, was eventually constructed between 1775 and 1779, with a bridge over Cow Lane, so that animals could still be unloaded and pass up the cobbled street directly into Church Square. But, behind the Coal Quay, lines of warehouses were soon built, with one or sometimes two storeys of cellars below road level: not many still survive, but Marquands' Ships' Chandlers is an excellent example. Further north, beyond the North Quay, now the Crown Pier, the beach remained as before. To this day, it is possible to see rings for tying up ships in the paving of the alleys by the Royal Channel Islands Yacht Club and in the cellars of the shops on the seaward side of Le

Pollet, for there were no buildings on that side of the street until the 17th century, the retaining wall of the road effectively forming a sea wall.

To north and south, shipyards lined the shore, many flourishing well into the 19th century. Auctions were held of timber when ships were broken up, and many are the buildings in Town and indeed throughout the island that have genuine ships' timbers in them, frequently used as internal lintels over windows and doors, where their large pegholes or trenails would be concealed by plaster. From Elizabethan times onwards, this was a splendid source of seasoned building material.

It was towards the end of the 18th century that St Peter Port finally burst out of its medieval confines. The occasional fine house had appeared in The Grange by 1750, but it was the laying out of the New Town – the grid of roads forming Havilland Street, Saumaurez Street, St John's Street and Union Street – in the 1790s that set the fashion for the Georgian and Regency houses which followed. Within a generation, magnificent terraces and individual houses had filled these streets, Hauteville had been largely built up, and in The Grange and The Queen's Road (renamed after Queen Victoria's visit in 1846), splendid villas and more terraces transformed this area into the elegant environment we still enjoy today. We are indeed lucky that so many wonderful railings, lamps, gates and balconies escaped the fate of their 'mainland' counterparts during the Second World War. And until very recently, favourable taxation allowed most of the fine houses to stay in private hands, undivided into flats and usually beautifully maintained, their delicate glazing bars and original glass giving them a quality all too rarely found in other cities.

It was not long before major buildings also began to spring up in what had been so recently fields and gardens. St James' Church was erected in 1816 to provide English services for the garrison stationed at Fort George, itself constructed from 1780 onwards with a bewildering succession of batteries and barrack rooms on the heights between Les Vallettes and Fermain Bay. The Royal Court was finished in 1799. Opposite St James' Church, Elizabeth College was rebuilt by the same military architect, John Wilson, whose stylish buildings did so much to set the tone of 19th-century St Peter Port. He was also responsible for the first restoration of the Town Church in 1822, and for the construction of a new Meat Market in the same year; of the adjoining Arcades and the reconstruction of both sides of Fountain Street in 1830; and of many private houses of quality, such as Bonamy House near St James and Springfield in The Queen's Road.

During Victorian times, building gathered an increasing momentum. Whole new roads, such as Victoria Road, came into existence, lined with modest terraces of much interest, and older roads, such as Mount Durand, Les Canichers or Paris Street were built up. Together with Hauteville, they give St Peter Port an unforgettable charm, mostly because their houses, respecting each other in scale, are nevertheless very different in detail. Efforts were also made to transform the narrow streets of Town into wider thoroughfares, matching the graciousness of the outskirts. These efforts were, thankfully, only partially successful. It is easy to see where road-widening was started at the bottom of High Street and the top of Le Pollet, but petered out in both instances. Church Square was created by the demolition of the buildings closest to the Town Church, and by 1879 the eastern façade of the market buildings provided St Peter Port with something approaching the formality of a town hall. By that time, the almost visionary immensity of the new harbour had been finished, joining Castle Cornet for the first time to Town and continuing an esplanade supplanting all the old shipyards right across Havelet Bay, whence a new road was in due course cut to the outworks of Fort George, where the Bathing Pools were created. This harbour remained sufficient, with little modification, for island needs for over a hundred years, until the massive extension of it to the north was triggered in recent times by the need to create space for containerised shipping, for cars awaiting roll-on, roll-off ferries and for marinas for pleasure boats.

Modernisation has sometimes seemed, in the 20th century, close to vandalism. In a generation that thought differently from ours, we lost all of one side of Cornet Street in the name of slum clearance, removing at a stroke a huge number of interesting medieval buildings. And a little later, the totally unnecessary demolition of the 'Elizabethan' house on the corner of Coupée Lane was only exceeded, we might think, in its mindlessness by the removal of the Ville-au-Roi manor house about the same time in order to lay out the fine suburban estate that preserves only the name. These were major losses. And the habit of demolition for redevelopment, irrespective of the possibility of new uses for old buildings, has been a hard one to break, even to the present day. The unique prison of 1811 is at present being dismantled and the outstanding market buildings are being unpleasantly transformed, even as this is written. The horrors of the new States Offices, abandoning the dignified envelope of the older building on the North Esplanade for the shapeless blot of Sir Charles Frossard House in La Charroterie, together with the third incarnation of 'Tudor House' in Le Bordage, form the most intrusive of developments that respect neither the scale nor the tradition of their surroundings. But on the credit side, St James' Church has been rescued and turned into a stylish concert hall, now accompanied by a modern building that does not detract from it, the Town Hospital has, after a battle, become a new police station of which everyone appears, quite rightly, to be proud, and a handful of brand-new developments have become real ornaments to St Peter Port: the Crédit-Suisse buildings facing Havelet Bay and Elizabeth House at the bottom of the Ruette Braye are perhaps the best. Run-down warehouses in Le Truchot have been replaced by various banking and business premises which, if they are not individually inspiring, are at least visually unobtrusive, and the Royal Bank of Canada in Upland Road also fits modestly, in spite of being quite large, into its historic environment. Elsewhere, marvellous buildings, such as the ironwork shopfronts in Smith Street, continue to be superbly maintained and the historic buildings in Castle Cornet have recently been much enhanced.

But it has to be said that the future for St Peter Port is not bright. The admittedly scruffy buildings that grew up over the years on the Gas Company's premises in the north of the parish have already been replaced with enormous structures, very impressive in themselves, but wholly out of scale with this part of the island. Thus the skyline of Guernsey, seen from the sea especially, has been changed for ever. And the new post office building further inland appears equally monstrous in its residential surroundings.

Fortunately, 150 years of photography have recorded many of these recent changes. It is the production of collections such as these, of which the late Carel Toms, sorely missed, provided several, that increases awareness of our heritage, good and bad. The infinite pleasure which Carel took in his island, and the concern he had that the pre-eminent appearance of St Peter Port amongst historic towns should be handed on to posterity retaining a charm that would continue to captivate every succeeding generation, is evident from the illustrations in this volume. One can only hope that a large readership will grasp the importance of being continually aware of the quality of its inheritance and of ensuring that it is not changed, bit by bit, until every historic detail has gone: rather that they will develop a pride in it that allows only the most sensitive of designs to be considered for the honour of a place in this very special town.

THE PLATES

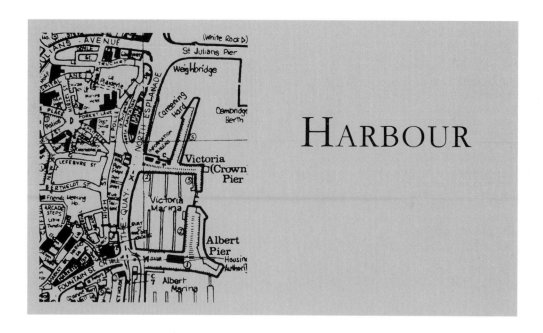

HARBOUR

The Crown Hotel *as it was during the five years of the German Occupation. It was then the Harbourmaster's Office. Before the 18th-century quay was built, its foundations stood on the shore.*

The start of a 'mystery drive' in August 1938, outside the States Office, which is now the States Tourist Office.

The Ship Inn *at the North Quay was run by P.W. Cooper in 1953. It is now part of the HSBC bank.*

The Pool in 1922. The paddle steamer Rescue *(the second of that name) was built for the Guernsey Steam Tug Company by Hepple and Co. of South Shields.*

Guernsey acquired a new lifeboat, the Euphosyne Kendall, *known as 'E.K.' in May 1954. Her skipper was Bert Petit, who is seen here during her maiden voyage from Cowes to Guernsey via Alderney.*

Brothers Tom and Jack Le Page, both fishermen, seen here after the Second World War. On 22 January 1945, they escaped to France accompanied by Frenchman Xavier Gollivet in their boat Etoile du Marin. *They took with them details of German fortifications and plans of minefields obtained by Gollivet when he worked in the German Harbourmaster's Office at the Crown Hotel. They also had information concerning the attack on Granville. The escape was planned by French Consular Agent, M.L.V. Lambert, who also obtained illicit petrol.*

The Channel Queen *alongside the Careening Hard in the 1860s. This was where boats were hauled up annually to be cleaned of weed and for repairing.*

With the Victoria Model Yacht Pond in the foreground the yachts behind are smaller than those of today. A photograph taken c.1937.

At this time, c.1863, the south arm of the old harbour had been rebuilt to the Albert Pier and completed at its east end as shown. It remained in this state until 1893. In the background work is in progress on the Castle Emplacement.

From about 1866 passengers could embark and disembark from the end of the Castle Emplacement or Breakwater beyond Castle Cornet. The ship here was probably the Weymouth, *a paddle steamer whose funnel is just visible.*

The old South Pier. It was demolished to make way for the new pier in 1859, when this photograph was taken.

The New Jetty seen here nearing completion in 1929. The first to use it was the mail steamer St Helier.

The Housing Authority took over a workshop (top right of the photograph), which had been erected by the Germans during the Occupation. Throughout the 1950s and 1960s fishing boats were still kept in this part of the harbour. Alongside the quay is Au Gre des Flots and Gratitude.

The Ringwood *seen here being loaded with tomatoes for Southampton from one of the last horse-drawn carts to use the White Rock (New Jetty) in 1957.* Ringwood's *capacity cargo was delivered on 9 July 1946 when she carried 61,564 12lb. 'chips'. In 1961 the Guernsey Tomato Marketing Board switched to using 12lb. trays.*

This picture shows what is now the North Beach car park during construction in 1984. After the sea had been excluded by the new wall the space was filled mainly with silt from St Peter Port harbour. Beyond the half-built wall on the right the Queen Elizabeth Marina *now stands.*

Until 1940 ships approaching St Peter Port were signalled by means of flags and cones on the upper battlements of Castle Cornet. The picture shows the signalman outside his lookout overlooking the harbour.

A supply barge arrives from France during the German Occupation (1940-5). The bunker on the north pier head was removed after the War.

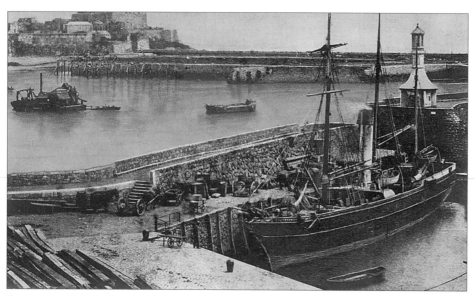

The lighthouse on the old South Pier was built in 1831-2. It stood on the foundations of the Round House which until then had served as a place of detention and a sea-mark, necessary because the jail had until 1806 been in Castle Cornet and prisoners had to be ferried to and from Guernsey. The lighthouse was demolished in 1860 and replaced by a wooden structure. In this photograph, c.1859, the new harbour works had not yet been completed.

The first hydrofoil was introduced between the Channel Islands and France in 1964. Here Condor I is seen in the harbour at St Malo.

A ship is about to be towed out of the Old Harbour having been unloaded at the quay in 1914. The tug Gannet *is standing by with steam up.*

The white lifeboat house was built in 1881 and Queen Victoria's Model Yacht Pond in 1886. As we can see, both lifeboat slip and pond are still incomplete in this picture.

(Below) An RAF Sunderland flying boat loaded with passengers was taxiing into St Peter Port when it hit an obstruction and only just succeeded in limping into the harbour in the summer of 1954. In the Pool the craft began to sink, but launches rushed to its assistance and managed to tow it to the Careening Hard where it was beached and later broken up.

Picquet House was 'erected by the Government, A.D. 1819', says a pediment board. For many years the soldiers from Fort George and Castle Cornet occupied the building. There was a strong-room for disorderly persons. Seen here in 1967, the Albany buildings behind were still new.

During the Occupation, petrol was available purely for essential services, and then only for Germans. Omnibuses were replaced by the horse and cart. This one was being driven along the quay at the Old Harbour.

(Below) The scene outside the Town Church during the Jubilee celebrations of King George V in 1935.

A view showing what became the North Esplanade taken from what is now the Careening Hard. Marshall's Royal Yacht Hotel was where Sir Isaac Brock, Saviour of Canada for the Empire, was born in 1769. Among the old buildings is J. and T. Snow Sailmaker. Reniers Hotel was later the Crown Hotel *(see plate 1)* and then the Royal Channel Islands Yacht Club.

(Right) The States Office seen here under construction at the North Esplanade in March 1912 by J.H. Duquemin. In medieval times the waterfront was directly below the buildings of Le Pollet, seen in the background.

Steam, smoke and dust – especially when the wind was easterly – typifies the scene at the Old Harbour (now a marina) when shiploads of anthracite coal were unloaded by hand and put into box carts for transport to the glasshouses.

WEIGHBRIDGE

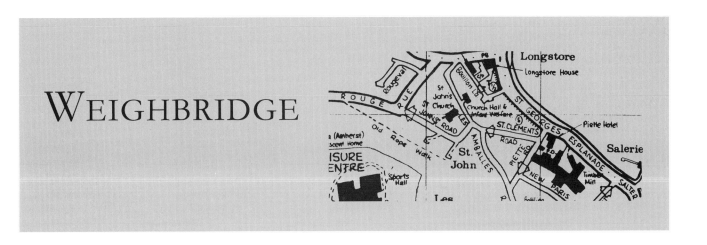

St Julian's Pier when the Weighbridge was just a wooden hut. The South Western Steam Company offices can be seen on the right of the crane (the last of this type of crane to exist is at the Castle Cornet Maritime Museum). Castle Carey, c.1829, can just be seen on the top of the horizon to the right, while Beauregard, of medieval origins (now Le Frégate), is also visible alongside its greenhouses. The Weighbridge as we know it today was built of stone in 1891-2. None of the buildings in the foreground now exists.

The White Hart Hotel *was a waterside public house opposite the Town Weighbridge. During the Occupation, the Germans converted it into a blockhouse and behind its concrete and steel walls was ammunition enough for blowing up the harbour installations.*

The bottom of St Julian's Avenue in the 1960s with the Channel Islands Steamship Co., on the left, the Royal Hotel *on the right and the Canichers behind.*

GLATEGNY ESPLANADE

In 1850 a shipyard was situated at the foot of what is now St Julian's Avenue. When this photograph was taken Spurways shipyard occupied the site. Later the owner was Matthew de Putron. The sailing ship between the buildings is about to be launched, stern first, onto the North Beach during high tide. The wall has been demolished to enable the ship to slide into the water.

Gardner's Royal Hotel, c.1894. *This was once* Le Grand Bosq, *the 18th-century town residence of the Le Marchant family. The annexe of the hotel, on the right, was later incorporated onto the main building and the medieval house on the left was acquired and rebuilt, forming another wing of the hotel. Note the extraordinary interlacing glazing bars of the windows over the main entrance.*

'Bel-voir', *which is next to* Wyndham's, *was the home of Her Majesty's Customs and Excise Department before that office was taken over by the States.*

Glategny in 1953. *Opposite the* Royal Hotel *a box cart is loaded with a great deal of seaweed which had been washed up on the slipway. The beach used to be the haunt of many sea birds until the 20-acre marina was built with accommodation for about 700 yachts. The hotel entrance has been moved to the left and two other buildings shown in the previous photograph have been rebuilt.*

The Channel Islands Hotel *at* Glategny Esplanade *in the 1930s. It was later renamed* Shirvells *after its owner at the time and then the* Savoy. *All is now demolished for new offices.*

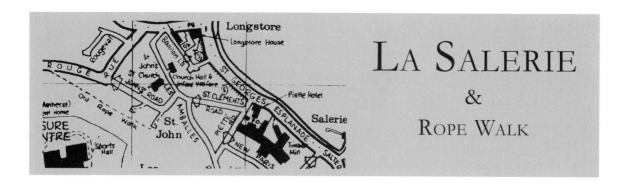

LA SALERIE

&

ROPE WALK

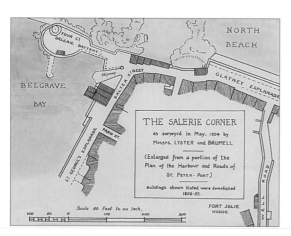

The Salerie Corner, showing Salter Street in 1854. Drawn by C.M. Toms. All the buildings on the seaward side of the street were demolished 1856-57.

There used to be houses on both sides of Salter Street. Those on the landward side are still there, overlooking the Salerie Battery. Fishermen in the 13th century salted conger eel here for sending to Gascony, where it supplemented the diet of those whose farmland had been given over to vineyards.

The Rope Walk at St John's around 1899. It is on a 100 ft. contour. It is up a narrow lane and stretches from a cottage where tar was heated almost to Amherst. The men on the left are teasing out the strands in preparation for making the rope. Rope walks like these are situated in various parts of Guernsey. The rope was mainly used as ships' ropes for the shipyards on the seafront at the Longstore and the Salerie. From left to right: L. Matthews; ?; J. Baker (foreman); J. King; G. Randall; and W. de Garis. The author of this book used to live in Rope Walk Cottage.

LES BANQUES

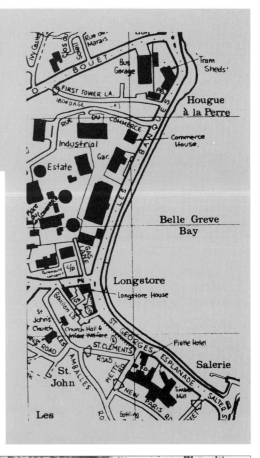

St John's Church, Les Amballes was built in 1838 at a cost of £2,600, and is a simple, granite church serving the northern end of St Peter Port.

Some of the Guernsey members of the Ancient Order of Foresters who attended an Easter Day service at St John's Church in 1935. In the procession is the vicar, the Rev. W. Kilshaw.

St George's Hall was a multi-purpose building. It was used as a depot for sending cigarettes to the troops during the First World War and was also used to store Red Cross parcels during the Occupation. The parcels were brought in by SS Vega and then transported to the depot by a steam railway which the Germans ran. It also hosted horticultural shows, boxing, roller skating and pop concerts.

The site of the States houses at Le Bouet in the 1920s. The gas holder was demolished in 2001, to be replaced by Admiral Park.

These four Dutch-gabled houses at Les Banques of c.1840 were used as cookhouses during the Occupation. As well as providing food for those in the area, they also provided meals for a few men stationed at Bréhon Tower in the Little Russel.

The offices in Piette Road, where, on 5 January 1830, Thomas Edge of London was given permission to produce gas at Les Amballes.

The dominant building in this picture is the 1971 Longstore House, built for the Co-operative Society. It was the source of much ridicule after Brett gave it a Z category in 1975 for being 'another sad and insensitive intrusion on the waterfront', at which time the Island Development Committee's planning offices were on the upper floors. Fortunately Brett has not recorded what has since happened to the rest of the waterfront.

The Fruit Export Co. Ltd was first established at White Rock, St Peter Port in 1904, and retained the premises until after the Second World War. In the 1920s the firm acquired additional premises at Les Banques. The sheds were used for the manufacture and storage of fruit baskets and flower boxes. This shed, which became the horticulture shop, was originally an aircraft hangar near Cirencester which was transported and re-erected on this site in 1921. The Fruit Export company vacated these premises soon after Christmas 2002 and they have since become part of the Admiral Park trading estate.

(Above) The brothers, George and Edmund Le Couteur, of Le Coudré, St Pierre-du-Bois, were tomato growers who also imported thousands of wicker baskets from France. The baskets held 12 lb. and had a lid which had to be tied on. The Le Couteurs had premises in Hospital Lane and another at Le Coudré in the west of Guernsey, called Les Banques, which is where this photograph was taken.

(Left) 'Martello' tower No. 1 was situated at Hougue à la Perre and was blown up on 2 July 1905 when the hillock was levelled. This assisted the tram cars on their journey from Town to St Sampson's. First Tower Lane still serves as a reminder of these towers, built around the island in the early 1780s.

HIGH STREET

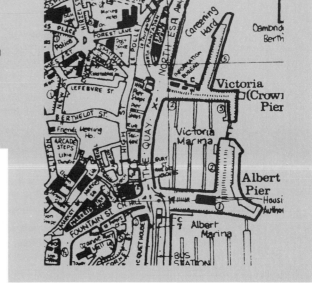

The corner of High Street in 1976. The curved shop was designed to link with the 1830s Commercial Arcade. Before the 19th century this area had been cluttered with other buildings, the shambles and in former times with the stocks and cage.

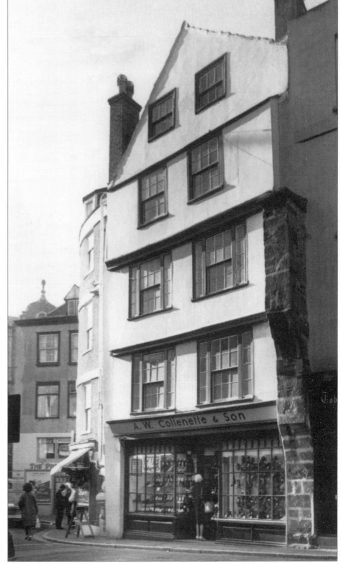

By comparison with similar features in Dinan, the jettied granite sidewall of this property is likely to be 13th-century, clearly intended for a building of only three storeys. The present frontage is 16th- or 17th-century, with later windows. A fine fireplace survived inside until thirty years ago.

The corner of Commercial Arcade where the Jewellers and Silversmiths had shop premises downstairs and a restaurant above.

A 19th-century plaster decoration over the windows of the Jewellers and Silversmiths.

This view, taken in 1891, shows the former Trustee Savings Bank, the jettied house on the right, complete with a timber-framed top storey which was later removed. Plans were drawn up in 1980 to replace it but this never happened. The stone sidewalls are much older, c.1500 or before, and there are vaulted cellars that pass underneath Berthelot Street. Before Jean Briard lived here c.1600 it had belonged to Jacques Monamy, who provided the earliest date on any Guernsey house – October 1578 – the original beam from the front of the house is now on the stairway of the Guille-Allès Library.

Nos. 15 and 17 Victoria House in 1903 was the thriving drapery and costume business of Abraham Bishop. It was later sold to Creasey and Son but continued for a while under the original name. Bishop's closing down sale was on 11 November 1930, when flannel shirts could be bought for 2s. 6d. and carpenters' aprons for 11½d. The picture shows Bishop's staff standing outside the premises.

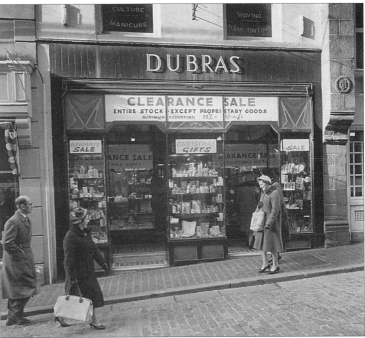

No. 22 High Street was formerly Barbet's Toy Shop before it was bought by Charles Dubras in 1928. It was taken over by William Deacon's Bank after this picture was taken in 1966. Note the merchant's mark of Jean Briard on the granite sidewall of the former Trustee Savings Bank.

Looking down Berthelot Street towards the High Street and the former Savings Bank around 1900. This jettied medieval house still survives in Berthelot Street. On the right the building alongside the children was completely rebuilt c.1960 and combined with the Bank.

On the road in 1940. The Martin brothers, who owned the tobacconists, seen here outside their premises during the Occupation.

In 1906 F. B. Guerin ran a mobile book and postcard stall. They would wheel it from their High Street premises to its pitch at the White Rock to meet the mail steamer from England or Jersey. On the left is Charles M. Toms, who later became a photographer with the Guernsey Press.

Lloyd's Bank was built in 1897 on the corner of Pollet and Smith Street at Le Grand Carrefour. The arch on the immediate left of the picture is the entrance to the Constables' Office, replacing the medieval entrance to the Le Marchant manor house, which had its own chapel in the courtyard behind.

The Constables' Office was built in 1787 by William le Marchant, Bailiff from 1771-1800, as a private house on the site of the medieval manor. It is interesting to compare this elegant façade with that of Moore's Hotel, some 25 years earlier. The tripartite 'Venetian' windows were formerly mirrored at another Le Marchant house, the Royal Hotel. Here the narrow glazing bars contrast with earlier, thicker ones in a tall Georgian house opposite.

COMMERCIAL ARCADE

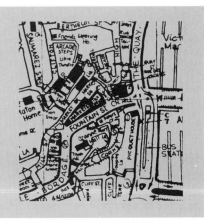

George Le Boutillier was a Jerseyman who came to Guernsey when he was 21 years old and set up a draper's business in 1804. He had been educated at Elizabeth College and was one of those responsible for its reconstitution in 1825. His chief claim to fame, however, was the creation of the Commercial Arcade with his brother, James. A vast amount of cliff face was excavated (126,000 cart loads of stone rubble) before construction could begin of the island's first pedestrian precinct. The rubble was used to fill in the South Esplanade. Work on the Arcade began in 1830 and was finished in 1838. There are cellars under each of the premises, intended as cisterns. But the project became so costly that the original idea of roofing it over was abandoned. The Boutilliers went bankrupt and emigrated to America. When the crash came about fifty houses had been built. Once complete, it was valued at £19,390, but sold for only £11,550.

The staff of Lipton's in Commercial Arcade standing outside the original shop in the 1930s. In the doorway is Frank Ephgrave the manager. On the extreme left is driver Mick Hamon, wearing the dark dress is cashier Miss Toussaint and far right is Jack Barrett.

W. J. Dye had a bag and umbrella shop in Commercial Arcade.

Part of Commercial Arcade, adjoining the High Street.

Taylor's Hotel in Commercial Arcade. The steps at the side of the building lead down to Church Square.

F.W. Coysh had a high-class drapery and millinery shop in Commercial Arcade. This is where the Arcade Post Office has been until recently (2002).

THE POLLET

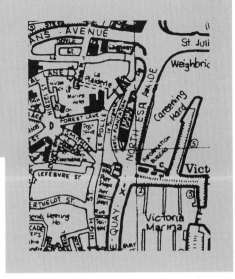

A fire in the Pollet in August 1937. It was at Delas' premises and drew considerable crowds.

(Below) Le Briseur's public house at No. 12 The Pollet in 1950. The interior was unprepossessing; it was dark, rather uncomfortable and had stone slabs on the floor. It was said to be the only pub in Town without a name. In 1951 it was bought for £5,200 and shortly afterwards was demolished to make way for an extension to a soft furniture store.

Miss Le Briseur at the public house in 1950.

A bearded 'Can-Can', otherwise known as Mr Davidson, was often seen walking up the Pollet in the 1970s with his twirly walking stick. He was a Canadian who settled in Guernsey. During the Second World War he was captured and sent to an internment camp. He died at the age of 92 in the Town Hospital.

Queuing for sweets from Collins' Sweet shop in the Pollet during the Occupation.

This charming bow-fronted building in the Pollet, seen here in 1911, was a sweetshop run by R.J. Collins.

C.A. Martin and Sons Ltd were famous for their copperware and particularly Guernsey milk-cans. R.J. Collins, next door, was well-known for its Guernsey sweets, made to special recipes.

(Right) Billy Rowswell, a well-known local character, lived at the Town Hospital. He was a newspaper boy in the early 1900s and amongst others sold the Evening Press, *first printed in the Pollet in 1897. He continued as a newspaper 'boy' for nearly 75 years and died in 1982.*

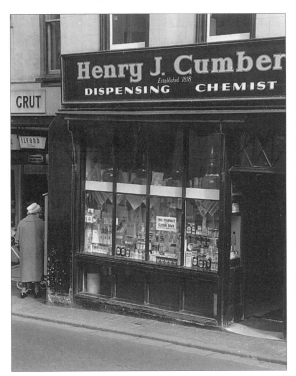

Henry J. Cumber's premises before it was taken over by Grut's in 1963.

John F. Le Quelenec was a well-known portrait photographer for Grut's. He started work with the company when he was aged 14 and stayed there until he was 69 years old. He died in 1975.

Purdy Bros boot and shoe shop was started in the 1930s.

Wilfred New was a street cleaner during the mid-1930s. This portrait by Norman Grut was exhibited at the Royal Institute Galleries, Piccadilly, in 1937. It was said to be by 'one of the fifty best photographers'.

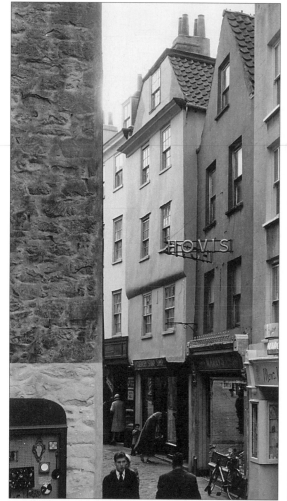

In the 1960s considerable redevelopment took place. This included the Guernsey Stamp Shop and Warry's bakery and confectionery shop, both of which were demolished and rebuilt. The former was clearly a medieval building in origin, with a 'jettied' or projecting upper floor.

Captain Tom Jarvis was master of several local ships. After his retirement he ran the Guernsey Stamp Shop in the Pollet.

Moore's Hotel grew into the town house of the de Saumarez, whose country residence was at Saumarez Park, during the 18th century. The splendid façade had probably been added by Matthew de Saumarez by the time of the Duke of Gloucester's unexpected visit in 1765.

Members of the newly formed Sarnia Cycling Club at the start of their second outing in June 1930.

The bronze bust of Thomas de la Rue, born in 1793 at a house still standing in the Forest. It was unveiled by the Bailiff in 1963 to celebrate the 150th anniversary of the printing of his own newspaper La Miroir Politique. Later, in England, he founded the firm which still prints stamps and banknotes.

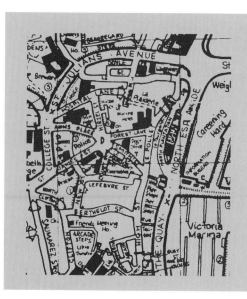

SMITH STREET

(LA RUE DES FORGES)

LE MARCHANT STREET,
MANOR PLACE & FOREST LANE

A fire broke out in what was formerly the premises of Lovell & Co. Ltd, opposite the Guernsey Press Office on 29 June 1935. In the foreground is the fire engine, Sarnia II, as well as numerous spectators.

Lovell & Partners and Maples were built c.1883. 'An exceptionally fine, rare pair of shop buildings with cast-iron frames and a vast quantity of pretty lacy cast-iron detailing, arches, pinnacles, rails and columns' says Brett. He also said, 'Both well cared for and painted. Each of the four storeys is glass, the window frames being decorated with a kind of arabesque filigree with a mosaic screen at the back of the windows, which has a very ornamental appearance.'

Boots the Chemists can best be appreciated by looking down Smith Street towards Le Grand Carrefour. This pair of splendid 18th-century merchants' houses was once the Yacht Commercial Hotel. *The plaque on the wall commemorates Isaac Brock who was born here on 6 October 1769. Brock was one of Guernsey's most famous sons. He was ordered to Canada with the 49th Foot and killed defending the frontiers of Canada against the Americans on 13 October 1812 at 42 years of age. At Queenston Heights a 210 ft. monument stands in his honour.*

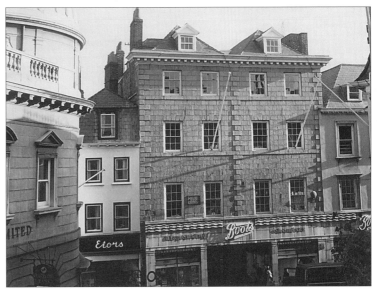

The Guernsey Press shop at No. 8 Smith Street in 1974. In 1979 the company moved its print works to Braye Road, but retained the Smith Street shop.

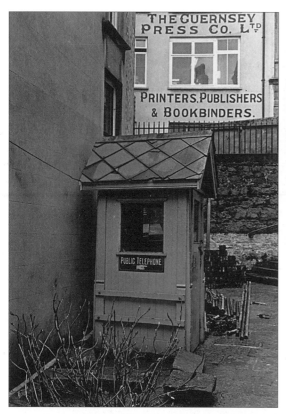

(Left) The Guernsey Press Co. Ltd moved to Smith Street (also known as Rue des Forges) and Le Marchant Street from Le Pollet in 1900 after the medieval buildings in this street had been demolished. This is believed to be the site of a forge which gave the street its name. The building housed the company's printing works until 1979. The telephone booth was typical of those provided when there was still a magneto exchange, but was upgraded to a modern version in 1970.

(Above) Lovell and Company in Smith Street were still functioning during the German Occupation.

(Left) The Barrieres de la Ville stone is one of six erected in 1700. The other stones are opposite Moore's Hotel in the Pollet; on the sea side of the Town Church; halfway up Fountain Street; and at the top of Cornet Street. This one is outside the Post Office in Smith Street.

(Below) This curious pillared stairway can be found at 19 Smith Street, one of three adjacent buildings of c.1840 which survived road-widening and rebuilding later in the century.

R.G. Davies, familiarly know as 'Jock', founded a successful travel agency at 19 Smith Street, now known as R.G. Davies Travel.

The former Masonic Temple in Le Marchant Street was built in 1882. Today it is a bank, but the façade has been retained.

Unveiling the War Memorial in 1926 in front of St Paul's Methodist Church. The church was later used as a social security office and depot for storing gas masks. Demolished in the 1970s, the area is now known locally as the 'Sunken Garden'. Old Government House Hotel, an amalgam of many buildings, is on the right.

Martin's copper workshop at Forest Lane where Arthur Russel is at work making Guernsey cans. Until 1960, these distinctive cans were used by milkmen on their rounds.

In Manor Place is this beautiful building, built to the curve of the street and long the offices of advocates. The large opening, on the left of the picture, was a stables used by Critchlow's the auctioneers and further down is the Prince of Wales *pub.*

The auctioneer Idon Critchlow had premises in a former stables at Manor Place. He is seen here conducting an auction in 1968.

The Prince of Wales *public house dominates this corner of Manor Place at the top of Smith Street.*

James Travers, who died in 1964, said he had had a drink every day of his life! He was the publican of the Prince of Wales *and* Coal Hole *pubs, one above the other on the corner of Smith Street.*

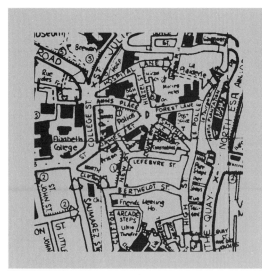

ROYAL COURT

The induction of Vice-Admiral Charles Mills, K.C.B., C.B.E., D.S.C., as Lieut-Governor in the Royal Court House in 1969, Sir William Arnold presiding as Bailiff.

The Royal Court House was built between 1792 and 1803 at the Rue du Manoir on land once forming part of the Le Marchants' manor. In 1792 the States appointed a committee to raise money by means of a lottery for its construction. The first meeting of the States to be held there was in January 1803. Substantial alterations and improvements were made to the Royal Court in 1822 costing £2,057 under the direction of John Wilson. Wings at each end were later built by J. H. Duquemin who also built the former States Offices by the Harbour.

HOSPITAL LANE

This arch and its surrounding walling, in Jersey granite and dating from c.1650, was formerly the entrance to L'Hyvreuse House, which stood near the Priaulx Library, from which location it was moved, in the 19th century, to the Town Hospital and its keystone renewed. The panel on the left, above the small arch, has the words 'Hôpital de Saint Pierre Port 1742': above the main arch is a Pelican in her piety. It is instructive that '1742' does not date its removal, nor the arch itself, but the founding of the Town Hospital which is seen behind, much extended in the 19th century and now used as the Island Police headquarters.

The Town Hospital Committee, with the Sister-in-Charge (seated on the right), and F.H. de la Rue, President (seated in the centre), in 1926.

Christmas Day at the Town Hospital in 1935, just before 56 men and 34 women sat down to eat their meal in the Day Room upstairs. From left to right: Deputy Marie Randall; Assistant Matron Mrs. H. Norris; the President F.H. de la Rue (carving); Assistant Master Mr H. Norris; Matron and Master Mrs S.J. Davidson and her husband; John Davidson (their son); Mr Cecil Stonelake (carving) and Miss Winnie Harvey. The building ceased to be a hospital in 1984 and it was converted into the police headquarters.

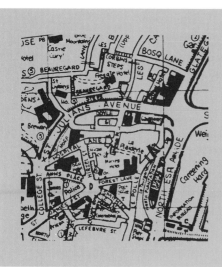

La Plaiderie

&

Sir William Place

These offices, which include the Department of Social Security, replaced the buildings in Sir William Place in 1976.

These pleasant houses, with tripartite windows from the second quarter of the 19th century, were about to be demolished when this picture was taken in 1974. The one above the 'no parking' sign was renowned for the china swan in its front window.

La Plaiderie, just off the Pollet, in 1925, when Guernsey's Royal Court granted permission to build 10 bedrooms over the old court house with a shop below. By that time the Court had long ceased to sit here, and the building itself was 18th-century. It was just to the right that substantial remains of Roman St Peter Port were found in the 1970s. In medieval times it was perhaps used for the collection of Crown revenues and comprised a building later known as le Cohu, suggesting an arcaded structure like a guildhall with a room above; it was here that the Royal Court sometimes met in post-medieval times.

La Plaiderie in 1996. The Georgian proportions are just about recognisable, otherwise the only original feature left is the flight of steps.

LE TRUCHOT

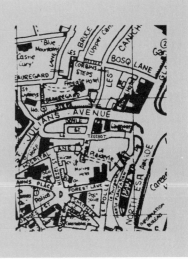

Looking down Le Truchot in 1974. The Cellar Club entrance was next door to Bob Davey's Garage and opposite, the centre right building was soon afterwards demolished and Wheadon House built in its stead.

The Cellar Club, Guernsey's first night club, was a popular place for young people in 1974. It was demolished in c.1984 to make way for a finance house.

These warehouses in Le Truchot, which had vaults for the storage of wines and spirits, were all demolished in 1976.

The first Methodist chapel to be built in the Channel Islands was built in 1789 at Rue Le Marchant. This Primitive Methodist chapel in Truchot Street, seen here in 1933, was built in the Welsh nonconformist tradition and was one of the last to be built in 1830. It was demolished in 1980, along with most of the rest of the street, to make way for merchant banks.

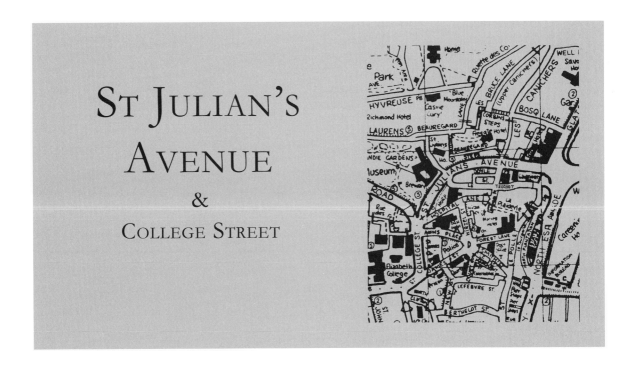

St Julian's Avenue

&

College Street

Looking up St Julian's Avenue with just a horse and cart on the road. The avenue did not exist before 1873 and the elm trees were planted in 1887. They were cut down in 1948 and replaced with maples and cherry trees. The South African War Memorial of 1905 is on the left.

(Above) St Julian's Avenue, before the elm trees were cut down in 1948, and, apart from a few parked cars, there is still no traffic!

(Left) Planting of new trees in St Julian's Avenue, 1948. Behind the workmen is C.P. Kinnell and Co. Ltd who were heating engineers and hardware merchants; the building was demolished to make way for a bank.

(Right) Drawing water from the lower pump in the Avenue in the 1950s.

One of the first films to be shown at the Gaumont Palace in 1940 was the German propaganda film *Victory in the West*. The cinema (built in 1876 as the Oddfellows' Hall) also acted as an air-raid shelter. Rothschild's Bank replaced the building in 1967.

The Palace Theatre, otherwise known as Billy Bartlett's, was also a favourite venue for such events as roller skating carnivals in the pre-war period. This one took place in February 1938.

One of the last coopers to work at Les Vauxlaurens Brewery was Mr Clements.

The pump at the foot of College Street already existed in 1770 as part of the Master's house at Elizabeth College. It became a public pump in 1831 after College Street had been created and when the depth of water was 30 feet. The St Peter Port Constables sank wells and constructed pumps between c.1784 until at least 1887. But many of the dates on pumps merely indicate when they were refurbished. The fragment of medieval arch alongside was once part of a Franciscan friary, whose premises were used in 1563 for the newly-founded College.

Motor House Limited was situated at the top of St Julian's Avenue and it was here that an Avro Avian aircraft was hidden from the Germans in 1940. The building is now offices, incorporating the buttressed walling of the old Franciscan friary. Straight ahead is Ann's Place, formerly known as La Chasse Vassal, and to the left the top end of Hospital Lane, which continued behind the photographer climbing the hill as the Rue des Frères, now a footpath. Neither College Street nor St Julian's Avenue existed before the 19th century.

St James' Street

The former St James' Church was built by Edward Way under the direction of John Wilson in 1818; it cost nearly £7,000. Brett calls it '… an extremely important and handsome specimen of the neo-Classical style'. It was restored by the Friends of St James and reopened in 1985 as a concert hall. The adjacent Dorey Room, once the church hall, was completely rebuilt in 2002 and now houses the Millennium Tapestry as well as a large range of other facilities. St James' Street was created when the church was built.

Honouring the war dead in the Garden of Remembrance at St James' Church, November 1935.

St James' Street, c.1850. The building on the left was built in 1888 and in 1921 became the first Police Station in the island. It was demolished in 1955 and St James' Chambers was erected on the site incorporating the Station and space for the Crown Officers.

The former States Prison seen here from within. In 1811 it cost £11,000 to build and in 1873 the States voted to spend £3,000 on building a chapel and new cell block, just visible to the left, and detached cells for females. All is now demolished to make way for enlargements to the Royal Court.

THE
GRANGE

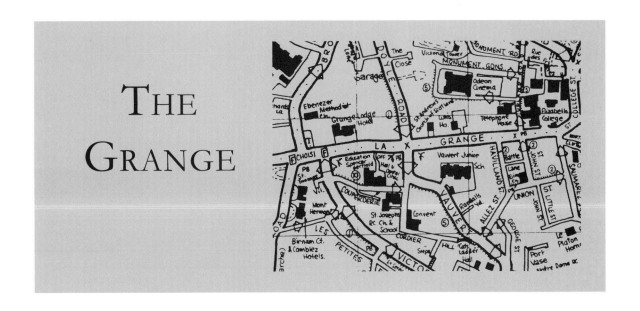

Bonamy House in The Grange, c.1820, a superb composition by John Wilson and subtly placed on a bend at the bottom of The Grange to be admired with his other masterpieces – Elizabeth College and St James.

The foundation stone of the refounded Elizabeth College was laid in 1826 and the building was completed in 1829. The original college was endowed by Queen Elizabeth in 1563. It is arguably John Wilson's most splendid achievement, with apologies to Walpole's 'Strawberry Hill' Gothick, all rendered in a buff-coloured 'Roman' cement.

The Duke of Connaught visited Guernsey in 1905 and unveiled the South African War Memorial in St Julian's Avenue. He is seen here driving up The Grange with the Lieut-Governor, Major General Campbell.

This Georgian shop on The Grange-Havilland Street corner, photographed in the 1870s, was replaced in the 1990s.

Lukis House, The Grange is an excellent two-storey stucco villa altered around 1840, only spoilt by the loss of its margin lights in one of the ground-floor windows.

This building, once in the garden of Lukis House, was formerly a meteorology station and is now used by the astronomy section of La Société Guernesiaise. It is now surrounded by cars instead of vegetables. Victoria Tower (1846) is in the background.

Roseneath was said by Brett to be, 'A good two-storey stucco house with a wide bow to the road, broad eaves, good iron work, glazed in a peculiar geometrical pattern.' Not only does the superb ironwork survive, as so often throughout St Peter Port, but the gas lamp on its elaborate bracket is intact.

Grange Lee is a fine example of a neo-Classical, two-storey Regency house.

St Andrew's Church of Scotland was built in 1887 by William Murray at a cost of £20,000.

The Ladies' College, seen in 1905, was here from 1878 until 1965. The house was originally a private house called 'Detroit' and was the seat of John Savery Brock, brother of the victor of the Battle of Detroit in 1812. It was built by his father-in-law, William de Jersey, early in the 19th century.

(Left) Grange Lodge Hotel *is 'A pretty piece of battlemented neo-Tudor nonsense. The arcade is ornamental with grotesque masks ... almost certainly by John Wilson,' says Brett. It was built in* c.*1831 for Charles de Jersey, H.M. Attorney General.*

(Above) Keppel Place, the home of the last Governor, Sir William Keppel, 1827-1834, has this rather curious plasterwork under the eaves of his former residence, another Regency house. Since 1835, Guernsey and Jersey have each had only Lieutenant-Governors.

Five roads converge at the top of The Grange, seen here in 1913 and five days after the States had decided to purchase and demolish Varna House standing on a medieval site at the corner with Brock Road. The horse and rider under the trees on the right of the picture are about to change with another horse coming up the Grange.

New Town

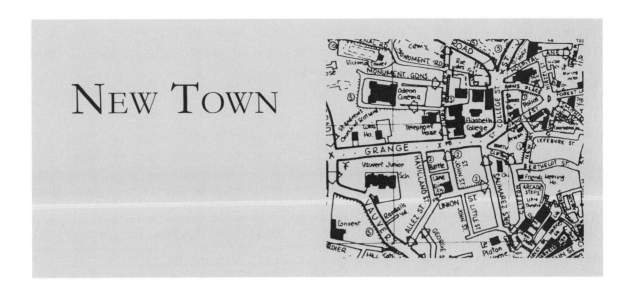

(Right) The builders' warehouse of Hainsworth and Co. in Havilland Street, c.1980, formerly Kinnell de Putron's Stores and originally built c.1800.

(Above) Originally the French Calvinist Sion Chapel, 1829-31, it later became the Clifton Hall, with the Salvation Army's motto of 'Blood and Fire' in vivid blue and cream dominating the seaward side.

The world's oldest working pillar box was erected in 1853 in Union Street and, repainted in its original maroon, is still in use today. The first experimental pillar box was set up in Jersey in 1852 followed by three in Guernsey.

The Eldad Elim Pentecostal Church in Union Street was built in 1831 and renovated in 1882.

No. 21, Havilland Street, is two-storeyed, with a double-fronted Georgian shop and a separate entrance for the householder.

BROCK ROAD

Melbourne Villa in Brock Road was built in the late 19th century. It was architecturally an odd house, with canted dormers, quoins, marigold motifs over the doors and windows, and strange curls in the cream stucco beside the window architraves.

George Watson was said to be the oldest cabbie in Guernsey in 1939.

A pre-1914 Victorian carriage of Charles Perchard of Melrose livery stables. The firm also hired out dog carts and saddle horses.

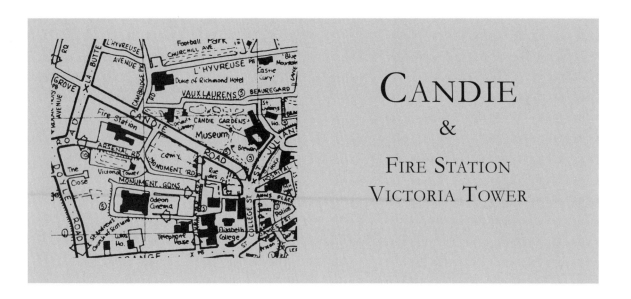

CANDIE

&

FIRE STATION
VICTORIA TOWER

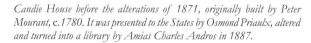

Candie House before the alterations of 1871, originally built by Peter Mourant, c.1780. It was presented to the States by Osmond Priaulx, altered and turned into a library by Amias Charles Andros in 1887.

Candie Cemetery with the 1831 Carey family tomb and behind it the Victoria Tower which was built to commemorate the visit of the Queen in 1846. Work started on the tower in 1848 from a design by William B. Collings of London. The builders were Matthew and Jacques Tostevin. It cost £2,000, which was raised by public subscription, and it was built on the site of L'Hyvreuse windmill, which had itself been on the site of a menhir, Le Pierre L'Hyvreuse.

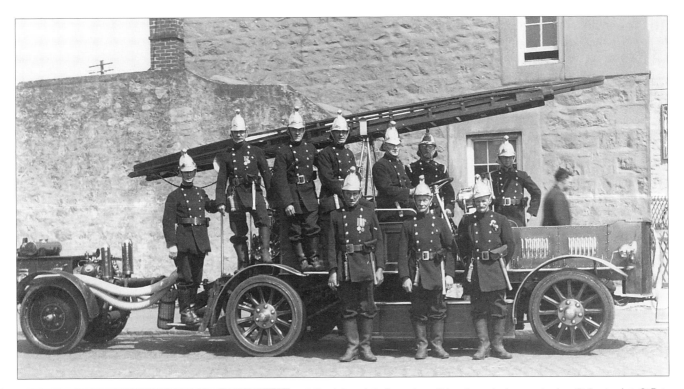

(Above) One of the fire engines which took part in the procession from St Sampson's to St Peter Port to celebrate the coronation of Queen Elizabeth II in 1953.

The bandstand at Candie Gardens, c.1900. In the inter-war years, this was expanded into a large glass auditorium, but there are still vestiges of the original to be seen, now attached to the Candie Museum and Art Gallery.

This is believed to be one of the first greenhouses to be erected in Guernsey, for Candie House, c.1780, now Candie Gardens.

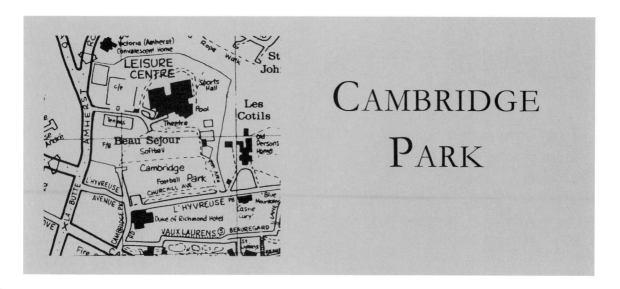

CAMBRIDGE PARK

King George V, Queen Mary and the Rev. George Whitley, behind whom is Sir Edward Ozanne, the newly-knighted Bailiff, walking amongst schoolchildren in Cambridge Park in 1921.

Castle Carey was built c.*1829 for John Carey (1788-1850). Brett called it a 'sub-Tudor Mansion of reddish brown stucco, with an impressive Gothick entrance'. It was used as an official residence by several Lieut-Governors and it was a German officers' club during the Occupation.*

L'Hyvreuse Lodge was one of a group of late Georgian and Regency stucco houses facing Cambridge Park and Churchill Avenue.

This large neo-Classical house was built before 1815 and was the seat of Henry Dobrée. It was demolished to make way for the Beau Séjour Leisure Centre in 1976.

This 17th-century double arch, drawn in 1815 for Berry's History of Guernsey, *was once the entrance to L'Hyvreuse House. Grover's Hotel has since been rebuilt as the* Duke of Richmond Hotel *(1970). The crest with initials WM over the arch has vanished.*

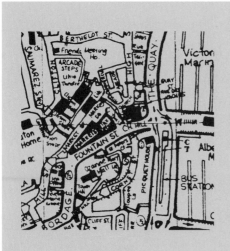

TOWN CHURCH

&

MOULIN DE LA MER

Business was hushed for two hours during the funeral service for Bailiff Arthur William Bell in June 1935. This was the scene at the Town Church where the coffin, draped in the red and white Guernsey flag, was placed in the hearse. The burial took place in the family vault at St Martin's parish churchyard. A.W. Bell was born at Swissville, Rohais, in 1868. He was sworn in as Bailiff in 1929 and succeeded Sir Havilland W. de Sausmarez.

Guernsey's first steam tram began to operate from St Peter Port to St Sampson's on 6 June 1879. It was run by the Guernsey Tramway Company and comprised one first-class carriage (here almost empty) and another carriage – open and much more primitive – provided for the less well-off or the economically-minded. Electric cars were introduced in 1892. The buildings in front of the Town Church were demolished in 1913. Note the wooden scaffolding around the Market.

(Above) The last tram to leave from St Peter Port to St Sampson's was on 9 June 1934.

The old Rue Tanquerel became steps after the Commercial Arcade was built in the 1830s. This photograph is taken from Church Square in 1951.

Hill Passage, c.1870, (now Church Hill) which led from Church Square in a north-westerly direction towards the present Market Steps. Here was the Moulin de la Mer, first recorded in 1135, the last of many operated by the stream coming down from La Charroterie. Below the mill was 'la grille', through which the water filtered and eventually found its way into the Old Harbour.

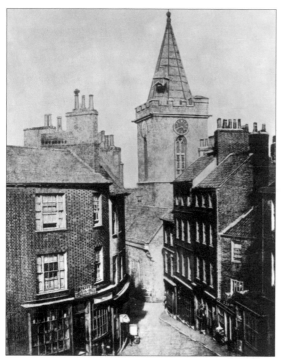

These buildings on both sides of the road were demolished to make way for the Bonded Store and Lower Market in the 1870s. In the background is the 13th-century north aisle of the Town Church, its angle splayed off to allow carts to pass freely. The tower dates from the middle of the 15th century, but the battlements and spire were not added until c.1500. The spire was releaded in 1722, when the outside bell was added.

Church Hill and the remains of the de Sausmarez House which may have been the residence of John de Sausmarez, Dean of Guernsey, in 1662. The section with doorway and two windows above was formerly at the head of a short alley, between buildings demolished in the 19th century. The white window sills are in 18th-century Portland stone, dating the large windows, but above the door and middle window are re-used 15th-century fireplace lintels carved with a merchant's mark a coat-of-arms with angel supporters.

THE MARKETS

&

MARKET SQUARE
GUILLE-ALLÈS LIBRARY

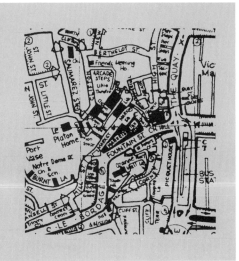

(Right) When John Wilson's Meat Market opened in 1822, there was, according to Brett, 'a formidable opening ceremony with a procession of butchers headed by a band of the Town Regiment, followed by refreshments'.

(Above) Queuing for meat in the Meat Market shortly after the Germans invaded, when meat was difficult to come by. The Meat Market remained much the same until the late 1970s when some of the stalls were combined and their original features replaced by the latest designs. The whole wonderful structure is now empty and about to be almost entirely demolished.

Christmas time at the Meat Market around 1974.

Opposite the Meat Market was the Poids de la Reine, or Queen's Weights, where all the fresh meat was weighed, seen here in 1956. In the 1980s the Poids de la Reine succumbed to the café culture.

In 1830 Les Arcades was built as a fish market. The symmetry of the building was destroyed when the Lower Vegetable Market was built. Originally it was 11 bays long; only 10 are now left in their original form. Up a winding staircase there is a very pretty pattern of iron rails, below which is a balustrade with a view of the Square.

Behind Les Arcades, an area was built by John Wilson in 1830 which held the Fish Market until that was moved into new halls in 1877, allowing this part to become devoted to fruit and vegetables. Now deserted, it is planned to preserve the 'internal street' within a redesigned shopping mall.

Madame Marie, as she was known, was one of the last French stallholders to work in the 1830 Vegetable Market.

(Above) Brett called the Fish Market, seen here in 1975, 'an architectural masterpiece'. The magnificent building was designed in 1875 and completed in 1877. The architect was faced with a very difficult problem, for Fountain Street and Market Street gradually converge to this point.

(Left) Looking west in the Fish Market, with its wonderful roof structure, during its heyday.

(Right) The Fish Market c.1974 (note the bulls-eye, louvred windows). White wood covers the original marble slabs, which slope and have a gutter, and are supported by granite pillars.

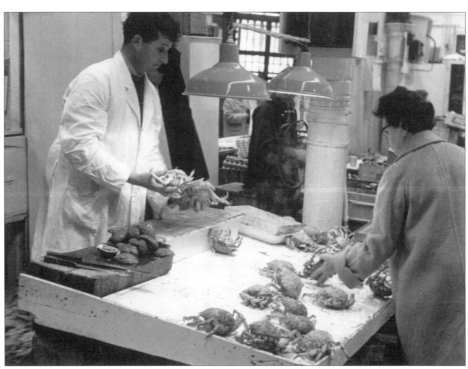

(Above) A customer in the Fish Market selects a spider crab, around 1976. These crabs are seldom eaten in Britain but are abundant off the Channel Islands. Note a small heap of ormers (abalone) on the left. Their gathering is strictly controlled. At one time there were about 26 stalls in the market. Now there are none.

(Right) A Lower Vegetable Market was first designed by John Newton, who had just completed the new Fish Market in 1877 but ultimately the designs of Francis Chambers were chosen and completed in 1879. On this site were medieval buildings, whilst Market Square was the Rectory garden. Excavation below the area about to be redeveloped has produced substantial evidence of Roman St Peter Port.

The ornaments on the ends of the roof ridges of the Lower Vegetable Market (1879) are bronze-leaved tobacco plants. They commemorate the tax on tobacco by which the building was partly financed.

The east gable of the 1879 Vegetable Market has some remarkably ornate gates with the Guernsey crest on them.

The Lower Vegetable Market in 1905. Amongst the display of bulbs, seeds and plants are some from Wheadon's and Vaudin's.

(Above) In the Lower Vegetable Market: the decorations on the capitals include ormer shells, pea pods and artichokes.

(Right) The Assembly Rooms (above the French Halles) were built in 1780-2 for the sum of £1,000 paid by subscription from the leading families of the day. The Rooms served as a setting for balls and suppers, being provided with a range and kitchen. The French Halles are now decorated by iron gates erected by J.W.L. Kreckeler in 1970. The photograph was taken through the upstairs anthemion-patterned iron rail of Les Arcades, above the Markets.

(Right) The Assembly Rooms – now the Guille-Allès Library – were finished in 1782. Later came the entrance to the library at the eastern end, which in this photograph of 1886 is under construction. The Post Office moved from next door to Mill Street before returning briefly to another building slightly to the right. This in turn has just been shut down.

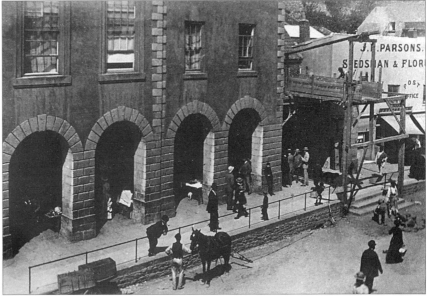

The entrance to the Guille-Allès Library, built in 1886. It has a great mansard roof with iron work and two bulls-eyes together with two-storey oriel windows above the main entrance.

A scene in the French Halles on a busy Saturday morning around 1974.

Inside the Guille-Allès Library in the 1920s. It shows part of the former reading room with upright wooden chairs and a musical motif over the west end. John Wesley preached here (when it was the Assembly Rooms) on 28 August 1787. Behind this room is the kitchen.

(Above) Looking along Market Street towards the French Halles around 1870. The first building on the left was the Hotel du Marché which had an elegant marbled pillared entrance. When the Guille-Allès Library owned the building it became an artisan's institute. It also had a room for table tennis downstairs and a reading room upstairs. It is now the Co-operative building. Notice, beyond John Wilson's 1822 Meat Market on the right, the final bay of his 1830s Arcade, which was redesigned when the 1879 Lower Vegetable Market was built.

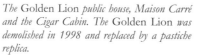

Door-to-door fish salesman Bill Prout discarded his baskets for a new, smart handcart in 1936. Here he is being watched by a small crowd at Le Petit Carrefour at the top entrance to the Fish Market.

The Golden Lion public house, Maison Carré and the Cigar Cabin. The Golden Lion was demolished in 1998 and replaced by a pastiche replica.

FOUNTAIN STREET

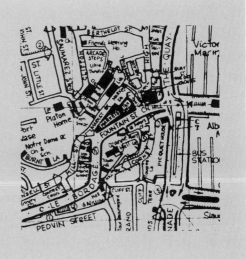

Looking down Fountain Street in 1971 showing the cobbles beneath the tarmac and Town Church in the background. Most of John Wilson's Doric columns of 1830 have survived between the shops.

A view of Fountain Street after road-widening at the upper end. Both sides in the foreground were rebuilt by John Wilson in 1830 as part of his new Markets.

Fountain Street after the completion of the Fish Market in 1877. The street was still cobbled and the upper part is awaiting road widening in a scheme devised by Amias Charles Andros in 1879. In the background on the left was Noel and de la Rue's household ironmongery business where Guernsey milk cans were manufactured.

A sign outside Phillips' the tobacconists in 1960.

The Wellington public house, which is part of the Market redevelopment, closed down at the end of 2001.

The Market Arms public house was situated on the left going up Fountain Street.

Outside A.J. Keates, pastry cook and confectioners; but the huge queue is waiting patiently for Pommiers' butchers to open. Both pictures were taken some time during the Occupation. The butchers closed in 1966.

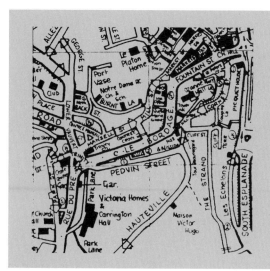

THE

BORDAGE

Le Petit Carrefour, or 'Top of the Market', as it looked around 1897, before the premises were demolished. Mill Street goes up on the right, Le Bordage on the left.

(Above) Austin House, seen here in 1970, is situated at the junction of The Bordage and Fountain Street at Le Petit Carrefour. It is probably part of alterations designed by Amias Charles Andros in 1879. In the background is the tower of St Barnabas Church.

(Right) A 1926 view looking up The Bordage during the road-widening that led to the building of the first Tudor House.

La Brasserie around 1926, formerly the home of the Carey family. It was briefly revealed once more in 1968. The loss of this outstanding building was a piece of architectural vandalism all too typical of the last 50 years and which unfortunately still continues.

The original Tudor House, which did at least re-use materials from the shops destroyed in 1926, as it looked in 1962 before it was demolished together with La Brasserie in 1968. Ridiculous as this mock timber-framing may seem, it was not so far removed from the medieval appearance of Town and was infinitely preferable to its two successors, the latest of which is arguably the most appalling edifice to insult the streets of St Peter Port.

These buildings on the west side of The Bordage were occupied in 1974 by Channel Communications Ltd, once the salt store. The second 'Tudor House', on the extreme right, had just gone up in 1968.

The north side of The Bordage in 2001. The following year the second 'Tudor House' was taken down, unlamented, only to be replaced with something even more disagreeable.

The north-west side of The Bordage in 1970. A salt store (on the extreme right) and Langlois' electrical business were situated here. It is now a bank.

A former wine cellar in The Bordage was converted into a pottery for a while in the 1970s.

The upper Bordage in 1907. On the left is a giant thermometer and the shop next to this was Martel & Son. The van going up the street belongs to J. Cluett at No. 5 Bordage. On the right is Podger the saddlers. Where the road joins Contrèe Croix Mansell was a corner shop where ships' biscuits were sold.

Walter John Ollivier the gunsmith (1874-1965) was born above this shop at 1 Tower Hill which was in existence in 1800. It was started by his great-great grandfather who, it is said, supplied knives, cutlasses, powder, shot and other items to privateers and captains operating from Guernsey. When grape-growing was at its height he would sharpen as many as 3,000 grape scissors every year.

Walter and Charles Penney, tinsmiths, at their premises on the south side of The Bordage in the 1960s.

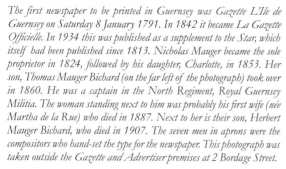

The first newspaper to be printed in Guernsey was Gazette L'Ile de Guernsey on Saturday 8 January 1791. In 1842 it became La Gazette Officielle. In 1934 this was published as a supplement to the Star, which itself had been published since 1813. Nicholas Mauger became the sole proprietor in 1824, followed by his daughter, Charlotte, in 1853. Her son, Thomas Mauger Bichard (on the far left of the photograph) took over in 1860. He was a captain in the North Regiment, Royal Guernsey Militia. The woman standing next to him was probably his first wife (née Martha de la Rue) who died in 1887. Next to her is their son, Herbert Mauger Bichard, who died in 1907. The seven men in aprons were the compositors who hand-set the type for the newspaper. This photograph was taken outside the Gazette and Advertiser premises at 2 Bordage Street.

Bordage Street and Pedvin Street (on the right). The house on the left has since been demolished and next door behind the hoarding was Henry's Monumental Works beyond which was a forage merchant. On the left coming up The Bordage behind the horse and cart was a taxidermist, who also sold bait, a basket maker and a coal merchant. All these buildings were demolished to make way for a car park, next to the surviving Victorian public toilet. The Britannia public house is still there.

On the right of The Bordage coming up is the pillared entrance to Brennan's furniture store. It has the arms of Andros, and had been intended for Les Annevilles, his house in St Sampson's. But before coming here it was purchased by John Brock and used for his house in High Street which became Burton's in 1934.

Demolition is in progress in the 1960s of the houses in The Bordage next to the public toilet.

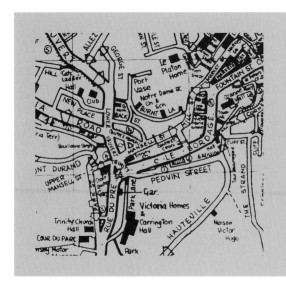

MILL STREET

&

MANSELL STREET
LOWER VAUVERT

There were no architects or planning departments around when these informal buildings grew up at the lower part of Vauvert. The shop on the right was where Paul Le Marquand ran a shoe-repairing business in Lower Vauvert.

Paul le Marquand, seen here in 1955, ran this shoe-repairing business from a tiny shop in Lower Vauvert for many years.

The picturesque alleyway between Upper Mansell Street and Mansell Court with a house built above it.

The early 19th-century bow-fronted premises near the top of Mansell Street. In the distance are the picturesque older buildings of Contrée Mansell, with the houses of Mount Durand rising behind.

Children at Notre Dame du Rosaire school enjoying a free, pre-Christmas meal under the auspices of La Société Française de Bienfaisance, on 19 December 1935.

Looking west along Mill Street in 1968, when the cobblestones were still covered over with tarmac.

Looking down Mill Street in 1982. The premises on the right beyond Blazes, where the Post Office used to be, was one of the many mills along this stream. Most of Mill Street, originally running alongside an open mill leat, is virtually level, whilst The Bordage, though parallel, followed the natural fall of the valley.

TRINITY SQUARE

&

VAUVERT
TOP OF MANSELL STREET

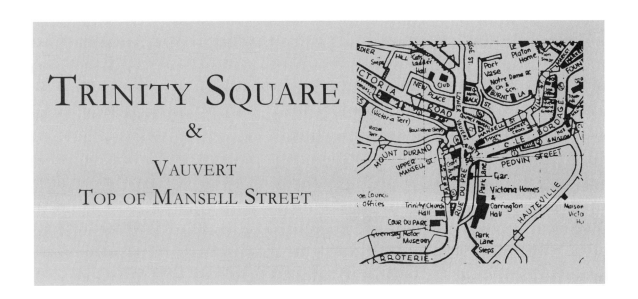

The southern side of Trinity Square in 1874, with Saunders Harness Maker, Saunders Shoeing Smith and Forage Merchant. The only thing left today is the pump on the right which is still in use. It is double sided: the side facing south has an enormous lion's head and a well proportioned trough for horses or cattle to drink from. On the back is a tap and hook to hang a bucket from. Sadly the lamp has gone.

In 1935 St Peter Port Garage moved into these new premises just around the corner from Trinity Square. The building to the right was replaced in the 1950s by another garage belonging to Stanley Noel. All were pleasantly redesigned c.1990.

In the 1950s, Trinity Square was dominated by garages owned by Stanley A. Noel Ltd. They replaced the two Saunders buildings shown in 1874.

Trinity Square and the church in August 1912: a scene of tranquillity without busy traffic or almost any parking.

Bouillon Steps, Lower Vauvert. Fears that these two old advertising posters would deteriorate and eventually disappear led the National Trust of Guernsey to acquire them. They are now in the Trust's museum at Saumarez Park.

Mr Walter Charles A. Watson, then aged 74, of Les Cornus, St Martin's with his horse Prince, was probably one of the last drivers to use Trinity Square. His cart used to carry many goods as well as taking tomatoes to the boat for shipment to the UK. During the 1950s Walter took Prince to Town three times a week in summer and once a week in winter to fetch coal and do the shopping.

The earliest fire insurance company was the Sun which was founded in 1710. The earliest Sun policy taken out in Guernsey was in 1723 by Thomas Le Marchant of Le Grand Carrefour from the premises at the top of High Street, for the sum of £1,000. At least one Sun mark exists in situ, on the front of No. 11 George Street. Another, recently vanished, was on the shop in Lower Hauteville, marking the corner of Tower Hill. A Royal Exchange fire mark remains on 9 Cliff Street nearby.

Maison Le Noury, now an art shop, had been a harness maker's premises. It stands at the corner with Upper Mansell Street (cobbled), Lower Vauvert and Trinity Square.

Mr and Mrs Williams with William Dorey outside their shop in 1903.

Les Caves de Bordeaux, Trinity Square. Unloading barrels into one side of the Square in the 1950s.

Les Caves de Bordeaux, Upper Mansell Street before the Second World War. It was then owned by the Feuillerat family.

(Left) Looking along Mansell Court is the curious upturned boat construction of Notre Dame du Rosaire in Burnt Lane. Behind it is the separate spire. The roof of 1829 was bomb-damaged during the Second World War and the whole church was refurbished by Père Lecluze in 1960.

At the foot of Victoria Road and the junction with Vauvert is this rounded building with 'decorations' where the gutters normally are. They are believed to have been some of the cargo from the sailing ship Liverpool, which was wrecked off Alderney in 1902. At the time she was the largest sailing ship in the world.

The lower part of Vauvert as it was in 1989. All the buildings on the left from the corner were demolished and rebuilt in 2001. The building on the left-hand corner was a blacksmith and locksmith.

The old house on the left in Burnt Lane, just below Notre Dame du Rosaire Church, was demolished and rebuilt in the 1970s. The steep alleyway on the right goes down to Back Street, but the path on the left follows the contours of the hillside and eventually rejoins Mill Street at the bottom of a flight of steps.

CHARROTERIE

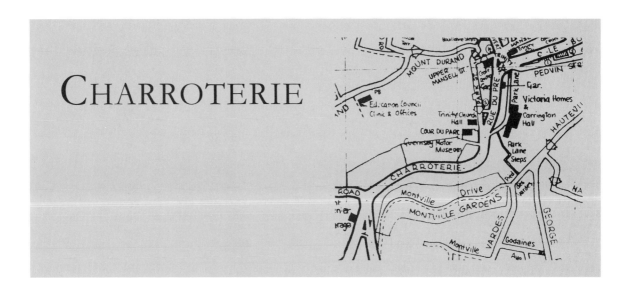

On the left as one travels up the Charroterie is the Chateau de Montagne. This is a fine mid-18th-century house, retaining some of its thick Georgian glazing bars in the windows, and, being on the outskirts of Town, was probably once thatched.

The Drunken Duck public house, Charroterie, with a 19th-century warehouse nearby.

The States' flats of 1969 at Cour au Parc seen here from across the Charroterie from Montville, with a fine panorama of St Peter Port in the background.

In 1935 an illuminated warning sign was erected here at Charroterie due to the many accidents that occurred at this bottleneck. The road was very narrow and the high wall on the left obscured the view, especially for the occupying Germans who found the corner difficult to negotiate with their large transporters. The wall was later demolished and rebuilt further back.

Looking down the Charroterie in 2001. On the left is Sir Charles Frossard House, the new States Office, with the rest of the Charroterie Mills' site empty and ready for new flats and offices finished in 2003. The small houses opposite replace Walden's Farm, whose cows daily went back and forth down this stretch of road until the 1970s.

Elizabeth House at the junction of Ruette Braye and Prince Albert Road. The old Lavoir Normand is just behind its roadside wall.

(Below) Behind and below the first gabled entrance to the former Western Counties Association is a pit where the mill wheel was once housed. The next two buildings along, the Phoenix Mills, have been supplanted by Sir Charles Frossard House.

Charles Ingram, blacksmith, at his Park Street forge in the 1950s.

These houses in Park Street were due to be demolished in 1961 to make way for the Cour au Parc flats, eventually built in 1969.

The Town Mills bakery is now a tastefully restored banking house, seen here before the alterations of 1974. Opposite is another warehouse where Keiller's manufactured marmalade: today restored as offices.

Scope Furnishing was the last building of the Charroterie Mills to be demolished, in 2001.

These houses were situated on the left at the upper end of the Charroterie, but were replaced in the 1970s by modern States houses. The photograph was taken in 1956.

This was the last washerwoman to use the lavoir *at the foot of the Ruette Braye in 1913.*

FERMAIN

&

SOUTH ESPLANADE

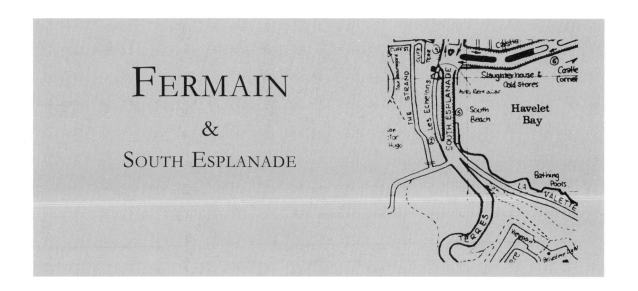

The vans of Le Riches Stores Limited on parade at the South Esplanade in the 1930s. The houses above in the Strand and Hauteville still survive, unlike the glasshouses on the right-hand slope.

The Guernsey Motor Cycle and Car Club, seen here in 1935, just about to set off on a treasure hunt from the Albert Dock, now the Albert Marina.

A horse and cart like this were often used to parade in competition at the South Esplanade, 1935.

The Farmers *public house in 1974 at the South Esplanade, opposite the bus terminus, newly laid out.*

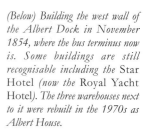

(Below) Building the west wall of the Albert Dock in November 1854, where the bus terminus now is. Some buildings are still recognisable including the Star Hotel *(now the* Royal Yacht Hotel*). The three warehouses next to it were rebuilt in the 1970s as Albert House.*

(Left) The South Beach in 1853. The contractor's mortar mill is indicated by the tall chimney. In front of the Star Hotel the level surface was used for making composite blocks of granite and concrete with which to face the new dock.

(Below) A tranquil scene on the Esplanade du Sud in the 1900s. The woman has to be in the picture to give it life! Most of the warehouses in the previous illustrations have already been replaced. The bus terminus has yet to arrive.

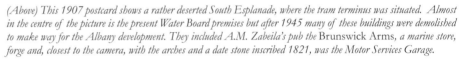

(Above) This 1907 postcard shows a rather deserted South Esplanade, where the tram terminus was situated. Almost in the centre of the picture is the present Water Board premises but after 1945 many of these buildings were demolished to make way for the Albany development. They included A.M. Zabeila's pub the Brunswick Arms, a marine store, forge and, closest to the camera, with the arches and a date stone inscribed 1821, was the Motor Services Garage.

These two properties below the Strand, and just north of Guernsey Brewery, were called 'Alsace' and 'Lorraine'. They were boarding houses but were extensively altered in the 1980s to become the Geisha Restaurant.

The lower end of Le Val Des Terres when it was being built in 1932 to give employment during the Great Depression. Havelet Bay can be seen in the background.

The Malt House, Guernsey Brewery, on the corner with Havelet. The date stone over the arch is inscribed 'A.D. Le Patourel, 1855'. The brewery closed in 2002.

The tunnel at Les Terres, now converted into an aquarium, was originally in 1864 intended as a continuation of the road along the foot of the cliffs to Fermain. On the left, Les Vallettes pool was opened in 1844.

Before the 1920s, when this was part of their estate at Fermain the De Putron Steps led to a private beach.

'Will they or won't they' allow a toilet to be built near the tea room at Fermain in 1932? In the end the Natural Beauties Committee gave the project the go-ahead. Little is known about the house in the background, which was practically demolished during the Occupation. The Germans used the stream to work a turbine to provide electricity.

Fermain Bay on 17 August 1939, just before war broke out. People often walked to the bay from Town or took their boats.

CORNET STREET

&

CLIFF STREET

(Right) La Tour Beauregard formed the medieval defences at the southern end of the town, as La Tour Gand (Ghent or Gaunt) did at the north. On its site is St Barnabas' Church, built 1870 and itself long empty though due to become the Inland Archives Office, and the position of its vanished gatehouse (used as a prison in the 1580s) is preserved by the street pattern, where Tower Steps, Tower Hill, Cliff Street and Lower Hauteville all converge to pass through it into Cornet Street. This Town boundary, outside which the inheritance laws were once different, is marked by one of the barrière stones.

(Left) Medieval and later buildings on the western side of Cornet Street in 1907. In spite of its 'gap-toothed' appearance today, Cornet Street was a very important street in medieval St Peter Port, already having at least 47 houses by 1331.

(Above) A new Town Church rectory was built on this site in 1950. Stones from the Cimetière des Soeurs were used for the steps. In 1935 the lower part of the street, of which most of the western side had just been demolished, looked like this. On the right was the Guernsey Pawnbroking Company at Lombardy House. In 1903 and for many years after the Clarence Hotel, the Customs House and Bucktrout and Co., wine and spirit merchants and shippers, operated nearby. They also had a cigarette factory there.

At the bottom of Cornet Street is St Thomas Place, forming a service road for the back of Fountain Street.

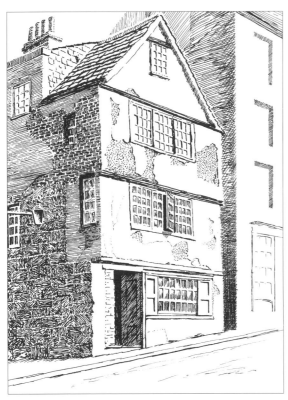

(Above) The 'Elizabethan House', no.24, was on the corner with Coupée Lane. Empty and a source of anxiety to the police but not in a ruinous condition, it was unnecessarily demolished in 1953. This drawing is inaccurate in that its medieval sidewall was not recessed, but jettied forward from no.26. But this clearly shows many alterations in brick, no doubt contemporary with 18th-century windows.

(Right) Looking down the south-east side of Cornet Street in 1905. All the buildings on the left went in 1935. The children are standing outside no.24, called the 'Elizabethan House' though it was older.

No. 26 Cornet Street, on early foundations, is full of fabulous 18th-century panelling. It was owned by William Le Poidevin in 1903. In the 1980s it was restored by the National Trust of Guernsey and is once again a working shop. The Regency bow-fronted windows have remarkable reeded shutters which open and shut by means of a handle from within the shop worked by turning a system of rods. Note the separate doorway for the householder.

In the parlour behind the shop at 26 Cornet Street is this example of a range by an unknown manufacturer.

The junction of Coupée Lane, Cliff Street and The Strand leads down these steps to the South Esplanade. The date beside the steps lower down (1809) records the earliest coursed rubble – as distinct from random rubble – walling in the Town.

HAUTEVILLE
&
PEDVIN STREET

A delightful corner of the eastern end of Pedvin Street, the two houses at right-angles now rebuilt, and showing the twin doors of Emma Place. Beyond is the house thought to have been the home of the carver Richard Guille (1806-1895).

One of the twin doors of Emma Place carved by Richard Guille. Other carvers of doors were John Burgess (1814-1904), Nicholas Robilliard (1817-98) and Henry Marquand. All made similar doors which are not found outside Guernsey. About 50 such doors are to be seen in St Peter Port.

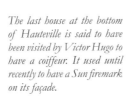

The last house at the bottom of Hauteville is said to have been visited by Victor Hugo to have a coiffeur. It used until recently to have a Sun firemark on its façade.

(Above) In 1938 Frank Blicq was the hairdresser at this gentleman's hairdresser. He retired at 72 from the salon which had been operating for 90 years.

(Right) In 1850 Victor Hugo fled France, first taking refuge in Brussels and then in October 1855 in Jersey. He bought Hauteville House from William Ozanne in 1856. He returned to France in 1872-3 and again in 1878 and his home was presented by his heirs to the Ville de Paris.

(Below) The entrance to Hauteville House, Victor Hugo's home, with the French tricolor flying.

(Above) The topmost room of Hauteville, where Hugo used to write while standing up, and where he spread his manuscripts on the sofa for the ink to dry. Included amongst his many works are Toilers of the Sea and probably his most famous, Les Miserables.

(Left) Victor Hugo's Dining Room. Like the rest of Hauteville House, the room was transformed after 1856 using recycled material, such as chairbacks for curtain pelmets. The ceiling is of carved oak, and the wall and chimney piece are tiled with Dutch Delftware. Between the windows is a carved wooden chair, dating from 1534. Of the various inscriptions carved by Hugo himself one is: 'Life is an exile'.

(Below) On a clear day Hugo could see the coast of France from this 'look out' room. It was here that Hugo composed some of his famous works.

The rear garden of Hauteville House.

A lunch for representatives of the States of Guernsey was held at the Gardner's Royal Hotel *by the French Government on the occasion of the inauguration of Victor Hugo's monument at Candie Gardens on 8 July 1914. The year 2002 was the bicentenary of the famous author's birth.*

Mesnil Careye was the home in Hauteville of the island historian Edith Carey, seen here at work in her study. The house was built by her ancestor, Isaac Carey, and is one of a pair of fine houses of 1785.

Maytrees, *built perhaps as late as 1845, as it was in 1974 when it was a hotel.*

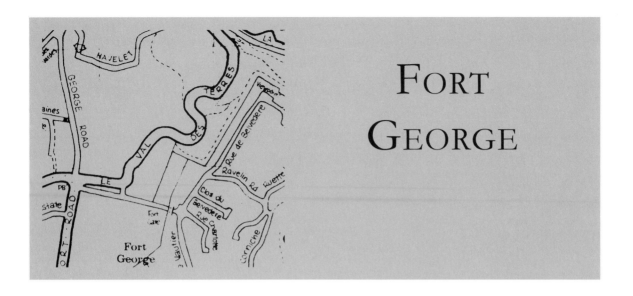

FORT GEORGE

Belvedere House, the Officers' Quarters for Fort George, c.1812, overlooking Castle Cornet and the harbour.

Building work at Fort George was started as early as 1775 but was not completed until 1815. The picture shows part of the ancient brickwork at Fort Irwin. On 4 June 1944, when Fort George was a German fortress, the R.A.F. attacked it and the guard room clock, inside the main gate, stopped at 5.25 p.m., the time at which the raid took place. The clock was removed from the original guard house to this position before being acquired by Mr G.C. Archer for his new house at Fort Irwin.

The guard house at Fort George in 1966, shortly before demolition. The National Trust of Guernsey was anxious to save it, but unfortunately failed.

COLBORNE ROAD

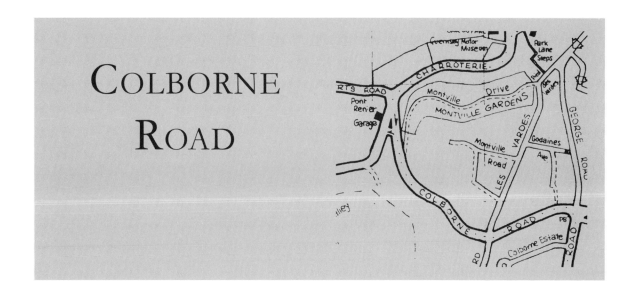

Some of the most outstanding decorative barge boards in Guernsey are on the gables of the Lodge at Montville. The original house was owned by Thomas Priaulx, founder of the Guernsey Banking Company who also helped found the Guernsey Chamber of Commerce. The house was built in 1800 and was situated near Le Pied des Vardes, but was destroyed by fire in 1911.

This panel, set in a projecting chimney breast in Montville Lodge, is a rendering of the Priaulx coat-of-arms, showing an eagle displayed and the simple motto, 'Caesar Auguste'.

La Colombelle, a name belonging to the field before there was ever a house on it, is just outside the parish boundary. Brett described it as 'High Victorian Exotic architecture, probably [built] c.1866'. It was constructed for Thomas le Retilley, who became a jurat in 1835.

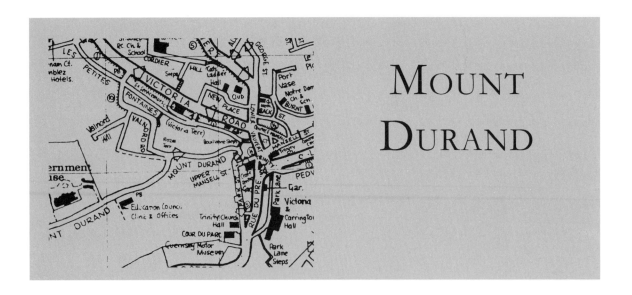

MOUNT DURAND

These curious houses, seen here in 1988, are at the foot of Mount Durand. The lane on the left leads to La Petite Fontaine and, via Bouillon Steps, into Vauvert.

Looking north from near La Colombelle with 'Rozel' prominent on Mount Durand. The house is still intact and surrounded by beautiful grounds and gardens. It was built by Thomas Carey (1780-1853) in 1804 and the name commemorates the medieval Fief de Rozel.

VICTORIA
ROAD

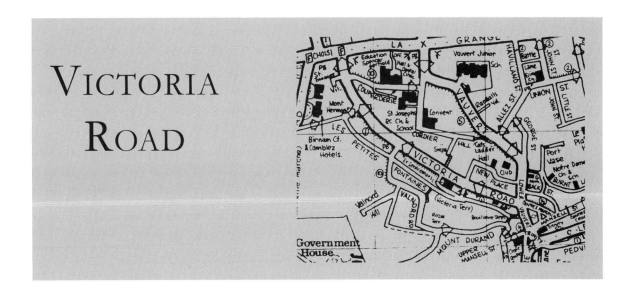

The view from Victoria Road of the Roman Catholic church of St Joseph and St Mary, La Couperderie, built by Augustus Welby Pugin. The spire was added around 1885 by P.P. Pugin and S.P. Pugin, and is 150 ft. above ground. 'St Joseph's is the only building Guernsey possesses by an international architect of standing and fame' (C.E.B. Brett, Buildings in the Town and Parish of St Peter Port, *1975)*

Victoria Road was an entirely new street, created in the late 1830s. Halfway along it is Emma Place, one of a terrace of houses with Gothick windows and façades of stucco over granite.

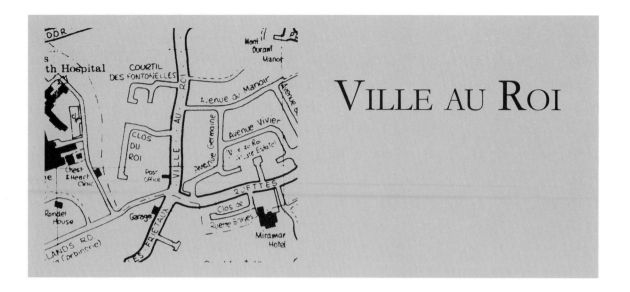

VILLE AU ROI

La Petite Ville, at the top of Ville au Roi, stood near the entrance to the Avenue du Manoir. It was an important house, even c.1300, when it was the home of Gaultier de la Salle, hanged in 1304. The blocked arch on the left could date from his time. The de Beauvoir family were responsible for much work around 1600, the date of the main arch and ashlar façade, and their arms were above a first-floor fireplace, now lost. The 'tourelle' or stair tower, with its gun loops, was originally 40 feet high, before being cut down during an 18th-century reroofing with pantiles. Seen here in 1940, its medieval structure in disrepair, it was finally demolished in 1953.

Road widening at the top of the Ville au Roi in 1933 claimed another casualty when the Travellers Joy (proprietors: Mr and Mrs Norman) was demolished, when the suburban Ville-au-Roi Estate was laid out. Beyond the public house was the Alexandra Nursing Home. The site is now occupied by Jeffrey's Service Station, behind which is the Medical Specialists Group building named Alexandra House.

THE QUEEN'S ROAD

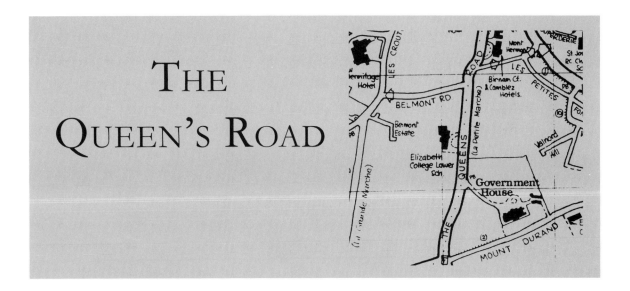

La Petite Marche was renamed The Queen's Road after the visit in 1846 of Queen Victoria. Here we can see 'Springfield' which Brett said could be attributed 'with some confidence' to the architect, John Wilson.

Government House was originally 'The Mount' and faced Mount Durand. It was built by Nicholas Mainguy in 1783 but much altered in 1881. It was acquired by the States after the First World War as a residence for the Lieut-Governors.

Belmont House is a fine, five-bay, three-storey house, built by Henry Brock before 1787.

Colborne Place – a pair of Regency houses. The right-hand house has been extended by two bays and its entrance altered even later, with a splendid carved door of around 1900. The great rows of slipware chimney pots, made at Fareham in Hampshire, are typical of early 19th-century houses in Guernsey.

LES GRAVÉES

&

ROHAIS

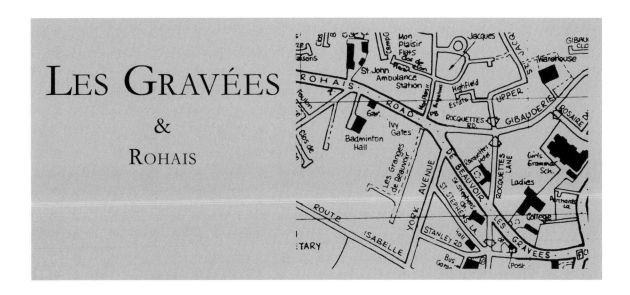

The 'Ivy Gates', Les Rohais, is shown here about 1900. This archway, partly buried by changing road levels, is now in the care of the National Trust of Guernsey. Originally it was at the head of a 'câche' or 'allée d'honneur', a driveway leading to Les Granges de Beauvoir, the island's most prestigious Elizabethan house. The larger arch was used by coaches and the smaller arch for pedestrians. On the keystone is the coat-of-arms of the de Beauvoirs.

The front of Les Granges de Beauvoir, facing south across an enclosed courtyard. The masonry is Elizabethan, but its windows were changed in the 18th and 19th centuries, and its porch was added during the German Occupation.

St Stephen's Church was designed by the architect G.F. Bodley, and built by D. de Putron. Its foundation stone was laid in 1862 and it was consecrated in 1865. It continues to serve the needs of the island's Anglo-Catholic community.

In 1935 a Christmas party was held at St Stephen's schoolroom, where the children eagerly awaited Father Christmas.

A horse-drawn ambulance, brought into use during the Second World War, is now on display at the Occupation Museum.

Under the inspired leadership of Reg Blanchford, OBE, GM, LFIBA, the Guernsey St John Ambulance Brigade was able to continue throughout the Occupation. Using a cheap camera and film bought from Woolworths, he also took many 'illegal' photographs under the Germans' noses.

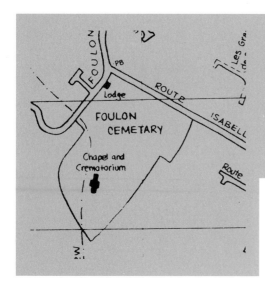

FOULON CEMETERY

In the Foulon Road is a most attractive chapel built in 1856 and standing on a summit amidst undulating greenery. Part of it was converted to a crematorium in 1926 for £3,150, the cost including a chimney disguised as a truncated spire. The original spirelet stands beside the pointed arched entrance. The roof is of fish-scale slates.

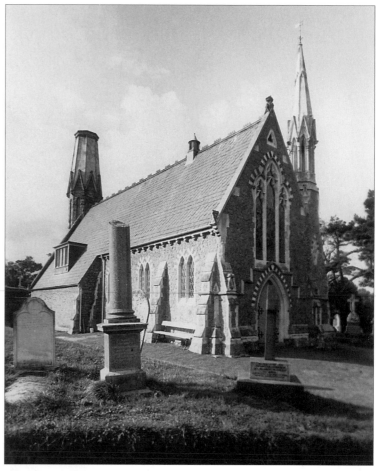

The gateway and lodge at Le Foulon cemetery, 1856. The remains of the original fulling mill, which gave the area its name, are in a house on the other side of the road.

FOSSE ANDRÉ

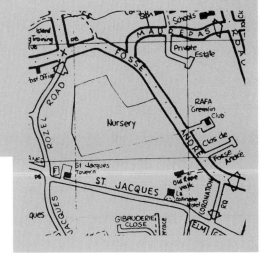

In 1863 Charles Smith started sending flowers to Covent Garden from his nursery at the Fosse André. He became one of the foremost distributors on the island. John de Putron (junior), the then proprietor, is on the right of this picture, which was taken in 1960.

In 1935 the Old Amherstians' Association held a party and hundreds of youngsters came to show their happy faces.

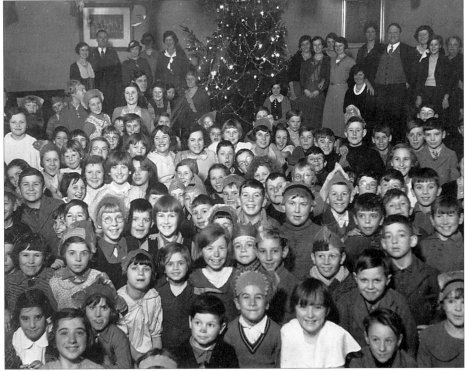

The Water Lanes at La Couture in high Victorian times, when it was really out in the country.

A box cart ready for the day's work at the Caledonia Nursery.

INDEX

compiled by Auriol Griffith-Jones